# Living with
# LDS Alcoholics

## TWO LEVELS OF HEALING

Memoirs by

## Trixie Neal

Fulton Books
Meadville, PA

Published by Fulton Books 2023

Cover design / artwork by Wynter Designs
Edited by Doris Foster.

To protect the innocent and respect true repentance, the author is using a pen name and changing names of all individuals, places, names of businesses, and some dates.

ISBN 979-8-88731-342-9 (paperback)
ISBN 979-8-88731-343-6 (digital)

Printed in the United States of America

Dedicated to and in loving memory of my parents
Nathan and Anna Hall

# CONTENTS

# INTRODUCTION

## Personal Perspective

The title (Living with LDS Alcoholics) sure sounds like an oxymoron, right? Lived it. This personal perspective is just that. It is my account as the firstborn child in my family with my view of upbringing and beyond. My interpretation may be slightly different from that of my three younger siblings. This is my journey of growth and falling but getting back up repeatedly. Without the Gospel of Jesus Christ's teachings and blessings, I do not believe I would still be here to share this difficult but miraculous story of the two levels of healing. If I can but help one person struggling with similar challenges, then the hours of writing this will be priceless to me.

# I STAND ALL AMAZED

Charles H. Gabriel, 1856–1932

I stand all amazed at the love Jesus offers me,

Confused at the grace that so fully he proffers me.

I tremble to know that for me he; was crucified,

That for me a sinner. He suffered he bled and died.

I marvel that he would descend from his throne divine,

To rescue a soul so rebellious and proud as mine,

That he should extend his great love unto such as I,

Sufficient to own, to redeem, and to justify.

I think of his hands pierced and bleeding to pay the debt!

Such mercy, such love, and devotion can I forget?

No, no, I will praise and a door at the mercy seat,

Until at the glorified throne, I kneel at his feet.

Oh, it is wonderful that he should care for me enough to die for me!

Oh, it is wonderful, wonderful to me!

# LASTLY

From time to time, we pray to know how things will work out, but we will not grow in faith if answers are given ahead of time. My father, Nathan, was on the high counsel and then bishop in his early sixties, later than most bishops who are called. At the time he was set apart[1] as bishop, he asked if he was the oldest bishop on earth. He was surprised at the answer. "Well, no. There is a bishop in Holland who is one year older than you."

At the same time, my mother, Anna, got her dream calling of playing the organ in sacrament meeting.[2] We think Bishop Hall pulled some strings there.

These were proud years for my parents (and their children) as they served in the ward in Lake Arrowhead, California. My mother changed the name she called my father from "Dad" to "Bishop." Growing up, I never imagined this would come lastly.

*The Lord said: "Ye ought to forgive one another; for he that forgiveth not his brother his trespasses standeth condemned before the Lord; for there remaineth in him the greater sin. I, the Lord, will forgive whom I will forgive, but of you it is required to forgive all men."*

—Doctrine and Covenants 64:9–10

1 https://www.churchofjesuschrist.org/study/scriptures/gs/s etting-apart?lang=eng

2 https://en.wikipedia.org/wiki/Sacrament_meeting

# DAREDEVIL GENETICS

"Andrew, don't tell Mommy that I left my car door open a little bit. I wanna see what it feels like to fall out of a car." I was younger than three years old when I recall my mother going into a small store, while my brother and I waited in the car. We lived in Phoenix, Arizona, at this time. This was in the early 1950s. There were no such things as car seats or seat belts. When I sat in the front seat, my mother's arm would fly out across my chest when there was a sudden stop, carrying out the human seat belt job. Well, barely.

It does not seem that we were in the car alone exceptionally long that day. And this was not out of the ordinary in the 1950s, I believe. My mother returned, placing a small brown paper grocery bag behind her feet underneath the steering wheel. I remember the clanking noise it made, like glass jars or bottles.

I found out what it felt like to fall out of a car quicker than expected! Who can get inside the mind of a young child? Not me, even now at seventy years old. The car turned onto the main street, and out went the young girl onto the pavement. OUCH! I was up and running toward the car before my mother stopped and jumped out to fetch me. God had my back that day as there was no oncoming traffic.

Arriving home, my mother treated me lovingly, where I had scrapes and road burns on my knees, legs, and elbows. It was a bit bloody, but I marvel that I did not break anything. My mother finished, she thought, with a couple of bandages on her oldest daredevil child. Then she vanished from my sight behind her bedroom door where my father was. The door was locked.

I am not sure if my mother or father heard their oldest child crying for them as I peered under the crack of the door. I was uncomfortable and needed more attention on wounds and my little emotional "boo-boos" as well. There was a smoky smell coming from under that cracked door and the sound again of clanking bottles. I had a feeling of confusion. I think I fell asleep there. Andrew must have already been in his crib.

I am not sure who to blame for my predisposition of genetic daredevil instincts, but perhaps my father. In his youth, he would ski on canals in Arizona, holding on to a rope while his friends pulled him from their car. And then on up to his mideighties, he rode a motorcycle.

When I was three years old, my father drove our car to a gas station and left Andrew and I in the car. I wanted to see if I could push my finger into the gas can metal spout left on the back seat floor and pull it out. Seems I was a slow learner at that early age! My finger went in completely but would not be seen for a while. My father could not get my finger out either, so he disconnected the spout from the gas can.

In the hospital, I recall a long hallway, my father carrying me over his shoulder with the gas can spout dangling down his back from my swollen finger. Doctors laid me on a cold table with a bright light overhead. One had a sawlike tool in his hand, and he asked me to point where my finger ended inside the spout! Seriously? Even as an incredibly young child, I recognized the negative effect that could have on my body part if I guessed wrong.

The saw went through the tin back and forth. Whew! My finger was still attached. They put greasy stuff, most likely petroleum jelly, all over and twisted the nozzle off finally! I was fine, and upon returning home, I rode my tricycle in circles in our closed garage. When I got hungry, I looked for my parents. Their bedroom door was locked with the smoky smell coming from underneath again. And the clanky noise was back.

Yet again, being left in the car while my mother went into a convenience store (in retrospect, most likely a liquor store), Andrew and I were both in the vehicle's front seat. We were moving the steering wheel, pretending to drive, and messing with the windows.

Andrew was able to roll down the passenger window halfway and stick his head out of it. Being the bossy oldest child that I was (already at age three and a half), I instructed him to get his head back in the car or I would roll up the window!

Being the younger stubborn brother that he was at age two, he did not comply. I am sure he wished he would have. His older sister followed through with her earlier threat and began to roll the passenger window up as Andrew screamed in protest or pain.

Andrew's screams terrified me, and I stopped rolling the window up. I was unsure which direction to turn the handle to get my little brother's head loose. Most likely, someone outside alerted the clerk inside, and out came my mother.

She immediately unrolled the window, saving Andrew's head. Then she got in the driver's seat, placing the paper bag with clanking bottles on the floor behind her feet.

These are the beginning memories that perplexed me and worried me for years to come. There were times as the four of us (children) got older that my parents would leave us with babysitters for a few nights. This did not happen every month. I know they loved us. We had healthy meals, clothes, and vacations, and we did typical LDS family things like going to church. Except on those few occasions during the year when they were behind closed doors or out of town on their *other side*.

Our church family must have thought we were out of town often. My mother taught Primary with extravagant visual aids. We would joke around later in life, saying she was the teacher who would chisel an ice sculptor to place on a white tablecloth. Being a fun young men's leader was a legacy of my father. They never earned scout merit badges but had some incredible adventures, such as rafting down the Colorado River. My parents' episodes of changing to their *other side* happened about four times a year, I am guessing. It could last two days to two weeks.

To this day, it is painful for me to say that my industrious, loving parents of the LDS faith were "closet-case binge alcoholics." Interesting that smoking cigarettes went with it, but only, as far as I know, during those times. Active Latter-day Saints have standards of worthiness to keep faithfully. Since this was not an everyday occurrence or even every month, the four of us always held out hope that "this" would be the last time of changing to their *other side*. It finally was…years later.

I am not writing to chastise those who drink alcohol occasionally or smoke. That is a norm in some very functional and loving families. However, that lifestyle for active Latter-day Saints is not the norm. My parents pretended to be "all-in" with their religion for around forty years. Hiding their attraction to alcohol while their children were neglected and given unnecessary concerns and stress—that is a huge concern and not the norm, even if it is only a few times a year.

For the record, I am thankful for all of the great memories in between the rough times. "Thanks, Mom and Dad, for allowing us the hope that can bring eternal happiness through the Atonement[1] of our Savior Jesus Christ. And thanks for the crazy daredevil genetics!"

Nathan's eighty-fourth birthday

Trixie at thirty-six years old

My brother and his daughter

My nephew

My daughter (flier) during high school cheer

Troy and Trixie on tandem at age seventy

*Who is righteous? Anyone who is repenting. No matter how bad he has been, if he is repenting, he is a righteous man. There is hope for him. And no matter how good he has been all his life if he is not repenting, he is a wicked man. The difference is which way you are facing. The man on the top of the stairs facing down is much worse off than the man on the bottom step who is facing up. It is the direction we are facing that is repentance, and that is what determines whether we are good or bad.*[2]

—Hugh Nibley

1   https://www.churchofjesuschrist.org/study/manual/true-to-the-faith-atone-ment-of-jesus-christ?lang=eng

2   Hugh Nibley, "Funeral Address," https://ldschurchquotes.com/hugh-nibley-on-who is righteous/

# TEMPLE-ONLY MARRIAGE

My mother was quite popular in high school. She was child number four of six. Her family was well off compared to my father's. His father had passed away from a ruptured appendix at the age of twenty-four. With help from relatives, his young mother raised him and his sister. She did not remarry until after her children were grown and married. My father said that could have been partly his fault because he would threaten his mother that if she remarried, he would shave the man's hair off his head while he slept!

From what my parents told me, my father was in the "tough guy" crowd in high school. After discussions with my father in his old age, I realized that the drinking most likely started then. He held many jobs, as most young people do, before finding his niche in California.

In between Arizona and California, we lived in Oregon for three months. At only four years old, I have quite a few fun and silly memories in that brief time. I do not recall my parents being locked behind their bedroom door.

My father worked at a plywood mill on the Rogue River. He used to help me find snails outside of the two-story cabin we lived in. I would cram a glass jar full of the slimy critters. Lisa was the baby then and crawled around. I can still picture my little sister slowly ascending the stairs as a mouse scurried in front of her, startling her! Another time, she stuck her tongue in a mouse trap that was underneath the stairwell, and SNAP! I have noticed there was no lasting effect from that small injury.

Our first residence in California was in National City and then later Imperial Beach. Before I started kindergarten at age five, my father was hired as operational manager for three thrift stores in

Southern California. Setting up our family away from Arizona was my father's goal shortly after he married my mother. He told me they wanted to be more independent, away from relatives.

One of the homes we lived in while I was young was across the street from a public pool. I used to go by myself even as young as six years old. Once, before I left to swim, since my parents were locked away in their bedroom (most likely on their *other side*), I snuck my mother's two-piece swimsuit from the laundry room and put safety pins in it to make it fit. Well, in the eyes of a six-year-old, it fit. I was excited to finally have a two-piece to wear instead of an ugly one-piece swimsuit.

I clearly remember the stares of many adults at the pool. One of the attendants asked me why I had my mother's swimsuit on. How in the world did they know? I waded into the nicely heated pool, and, at once, something strange happened. I had to leave pretty quickly as my attire stretched out upon water contact!

While living in this same house, after my youngest brother was born, we had a housekeeper or nanny, if I remember correctly. I wanted to sell my amazing newspaper-folded hats to neighbors that I knew would make a lot of money! Again, through the mind of a six-year-old. The young gal holding my baby brother told me I had to stay home. But I knocked on my parents' door and told them what I wanted to do. Receiving the "okay" I left and began knocking on about eight neighbors' front doors. I was bewildered as to why none of them wanted to buy the elaborate newspaper hats, the only ones like them in the world! I did get a nickel from one neighbor, but he told me to keep my hats for myself.

In both of these situations, there are so many things that could have happened to me as a young child. I would not have allowed my children to go alone to a pool or sell door-to-door. And those are only a couple of memories of something that could have gone terribly wrong. Supervision is key to keeping young children safe. Thankfully, God had my back.

As a result of my mother's laid-back nature, she was always running late. I knew my father would become irritated as we drove to church late again. She would be looking out the passenger window with tears in her eyes as her husband stomped on the gas pedal. After my mother passed away, he regretted not helping her get their four children ready or putting dinner in the oven, slow cooking to be ready upon our return. It seems these were the times of our history when mothers took care of the children and home. Fathers worked and earned a living. This left its mark on me, as I need to be punctual and organized with my time. I have the drive to be independent and am not afraid to ask for help from my husband.

As a child and on up, my parents did not talk about reasons to go to the temple besides to get married. I learned other reasons, such as proxy work to bless those who have passed away, during young women's lessons.

My parents never attended the temple until one of my brothers was married there and then me and then my younger brother. I heard how that changed after their move to Lake Arrowhead upon my father's retirement. "Oh, it is wonderful."

My father's mother was active in the LDS church, as well as my mother's parents, who insisted and expected that their six children be married in the temple. When my father went to his future father-in-law and explained that they were going to have a civil ceremony and then, in about one year, go to the Mesa Temple, his reply was, "Temple marriage, my young man or no marriage!" My father says that was the smartest thing anyone ever told him or forced him to do. He had such gratitude for that later in life. I am grateful for my grandfather's testimony and for my parents raising me with the Gospel of Jesus Christ in my life.

15

*The Lord in His wisdom has warned us that substances that are not good for us should be totally avoided. We have been warned not to take the first drink, smoke the first cigarette, or try the first drug. Curiosity and peer pressure are selfish reasons to dabble with addictive substances. We should stop and consider the full consequences, not just to ourselves and our futures, but also to our loved ones. These consequences are physical, but they also risk the loss of the Spirit and cause us to fall prey to Satan.*[1]

—James E. Faust

1   James E. Faust, "A Royal Priesthood," April 2006 LDS General Conference https://www.google.com/search?q=james+e+faust+a+royal+priesthood&oq=-james+e+faust+a+royal+priesthood&aqs =chrome.69i57.15252j0j7&sourceid= chrome&ie=UTF-8

# RANCH HIDEAWAY

My parents liked to pack boxes, load, and unload furniture, it seemed. We moved more often than "army brats," I knew. The only time we did not move in less than two years, I believe, was when I was in third through seventh grade. That was a home they owned, and my father told me they always regretted selling that property because it would be worth over a million. It was a corner lot in Imperial Beach and a rockin neighborhood for us kids. My younger brother Rick told me once, when our mother announced to him it was time to pack his things in boxes because we were moving, he replied snidely, "No, I'm not packing boxes." She reminded him that to load up and move, things needed to be in boxes. His rebuttal was, "I never unpacked."

These were treasured days (for the most part). The children in this neighborhood could safely play outside in anyone's front or backyard, such as hide-and-seek. We only went inside of our house to eat or use the bathroom.

In the summer, we had an aboveground swimming pool that all of our friends could join us in. If my parents were out of town or behind their locked bedroom door, we would not have company because that would be embarrassing. I am not sure if anyone else knew of our parents' *other side*. As mentioned before, this only happened occasionally, so I doubt anyone was suspicious (unless they saw them elsewhere). I do not recall ever needing groceries at this age (eight to thirteen years old), and I could make sandwiches for my siblings.

Our parents always made sure we had a jam-packed Christmas. We normally said prayers to bless our meals and, every now and then, had family prayers. But I do not remember speaking about the birth of Christ or His life often or reading scriptures with them, so opening all the gifts seemed hypocritical to me. But as a young child, it was still fun to get all that stuff. It would turn out that most of our friends in our neighborhood would get similar toys that we did, so it would be a day to play and play and play, be it walkie-talkies, skateboards, bicycles, roller skates.

My parents had bought (or rented) a second home or getaway about fifteen miles away that they called "the Ranch." We had no TV or telephone there. It was an old place up in the hills without neighbors. My father would drive us there in the back of his pickup truck, and we had a blast. There was no fear in those days of falling out of the bed of a truck. Later, as a parent, I would not allow my children to do that, ever! (although I am sure some did anyway). We had fun at the Ranch, hiking around, throwing rocks at a falling-apart old building nearby, and shooting BB guns. My father taught us how to hunt rabbits. That was good eating when my mother fried them up.

After sixth grade, I had a boyfriend, and they let him come to the Ranch once overnight. I was fully developed but had no clue what sex was. My mother assumed I was taught at school. I told my boyfriend he could sleep in my bed, and he busted up laughing! Of course, he did not sleep with me, and he thought I had been joking. After that, I had to ask my mother how babies were made. As she described the "act," I was appalled. Seems back then, many parents did not instruct their children about important matters until much later than needed. I would have never believed then if someone had told me I would be having a family of eight children.

This ranch became a great getaway for my parents when they altered to their *other side*. I hated that intensely because we never knew if this was for two days or longer. We could not call them, and that was too far to skate or bike to. What good would that have done anyway?

At first, when our parents were MIA, we enjoyed it. The four of us could play outside however late we wanted to or have any friends over. Of course, we were careful, not knowing when our parents would return home.

I remember one weekend when I was in seventh grade, and they had not come home. It was Monday morning, a school day. The four of us usually walked to our schools. My three siblings went to an elementary school about eight blocks away, and my junior high was a little bit farther in a different direction. In those days, the late 1960s, there was no such term as anxiety or PTSD, but I know I had all the symptoms that morning and many others.

I made everyone's school lunch, then my three siblings left to walk to their elementary school. I walked alone to the junior high, holding back worried tears. The unknown in these types of situations was so frightening to me as a young teenager.

While sitting in my second-hour class, geography, I remember my queasy stomach feeling with thoughts of troubling questions such as, *What if my parents had died?* Before the end of class, a lady from the office came in and spoke with the teacher, who pointed to me. I was handed a note that said something like this: "Your parents called and said they are fine." Relief, yes. Anger? Absolutely!

Returning home from school, my mother did not apologize and acted like nothing had happened, completely indifferent. I was certainly not up to discussing it as it would bring back the feelings of wanting to vomit. My father was at work and returned home later to his warmly cooked dinner. So one more incident of my parents changing to their *other side*, which could be the last of its kind. We always hoped for that. It took years.

*Christmas is a time for remembering the Son of God and renewing our determination to take upon us his name. It is a time to reassess our lives and examine our thoughts, feelings, and actions. Let this be a time of remembrance, of gratitude and a time of forgiveness. Let it be a time to ponder the Atonement of Jesus Christ and its meaning for each of us personally. Let it especially be a time of renewal and recommitment to live by the word of God and to obey his commandments. By doing this, we honor him far more than we ever could with lights, gifts, or parties.*[1]

—Dieter F. Uchtdorf

[1] Elder Dieter F. Uchtdorf, "Seeing Christmas through New Eyes," https://m.facebook.com/dieterf.uchtdorf/posts/11040461997 66056

# ROLLER-SKATING ADDICTION

When I was six years old, I received my first pair of roller skates which were attached to my shoes. Our short sidewalk in front of our house was full of cracks and bumps. But I still found it thrilling.

When I turned twelve years old, my parents gave me my first pair of indoor rink roller skates. By this time, the four of us were going skating at least once a week at the roller-skating rink in Imperial Beach. These occasions were something in our life to look forward to for years to come. The Sweetwater Rink pulled us in with speed skating a few years later.

We made new friends there who are still in our life mainly via social media. The four of us got into racing, freestyle, and dance. We must have burned thousands of calories every time. And even more calories during the all-day skates, which went from noon to midnight. Sometimes we would take a break and walk up the street to a Mexican restaurant. Seems skating was the biggest part of our lives then, and the music made it even more fun. To this day, I rarely exercise without music.

Only once did my father come for a short while to skate—at least he called it skating. We were laughing hysterically as he slowly strode with his pants pulled up past his waist and his large bundle of work keys dangling noisily from his belt loop. I think now how brave that was of him!

Since Rick was the youngest and also talented, the skating instructors could see he had the potential to win competitions. My parents paid for Rick to have private instruction. I think the rest of us were a bit envious.

My parents had him compete only for a brief time, even though he always placed first in his age group. It involved traveling, which

I now realize my parents could not fully commit to. They would change to their *other side* sometimes and be MIA.

For me, these roller rink years lasted about six. I thrived on the competition, which boosted my self-esteem, and I enjoyed the friendships. I had less friends at school to begin with because of the different social classes back then and the fact that we moved a lot. Popularity was established at the rink because we did not look down on anyone. It was all about having fun. I remember when our school would have a skate night, and I would blow them all away with my speed, freestyle, and backward skating. Although I do not recall any of them mentioning it. But, I admit, it was fun to show off!

My parents always took us to the skating rink but did not always pick us up. After the last session which ended at midnight, the four of us would pick up our skates and saunter outside to see if our family station wagon or the yellow vehicle was there. And whenever that embarrassing yellow taxi pulled up, that answered our question if our mother and father had changed to their *other side* again. Our friends would just laugh, thinking our parents had gone to bed early. My head hung low all the way home. I would have admitted even then that there are bad addictions as well as good ones, such as roller skating.

I recently asked Rick if he remembered how we paid for all those taxi rides. He had no clue, but said he always enjoyed sitting in the front and sharing the taxicab driver's food. He especially remembers the delicious shrimp!

*Forgiveness is not an occasional act; it is a constant attitude.*[1]

—Martin Luther King Jr.

[1] Martin Luther King Jr., https://www.goodreads.com/quotes/57037-forgive-ness-is-not-an-occasional-act-it-is-a-constant

25

# DIAGNOSIS SHOCK

At the beginning of sixth grade, serious health issues arose for me. One evening I had an intense bloody nose while I slept. This came after I had mentioned to my parents that I thought I needed glasses because I could barely see out of one eye. They did not take me that serious as I had had a vision exam a few months earlier with a twenty-twenty result.

As long as I could remember, I had extreme allergies with a constant runny nose, and I would break out in hives sometimes. But upon my insistence, my mother took me back to the optometrist. After the exam, he seemed quite concerned that there could be pressure on an optic nerve and recommended I see an ophthalmologist as soon as possible.

After the specialists, including an ear, nose, and throat doctor, and x-rays, my parents were told that their oldest daughter had a tumor behind her eyes and sinuses that winded back near the stem of her brain. I was admitted to the hospital shortly afterward to undergo biopsy surgery. I was now twelve years old.

None of my children have ever had anything that serious. It must have caused intense concern for my parents. I imagine they prayed more fervently than they ever had. I remember a priesthood blessing[1] our bishop gave me before my first of several surgeries. In the blessing, he promised that the impurities would flow with the blood. The only reason I recall this was my parents were discussing what he had said afterward, and they seemed bothered and puzzled by it.

In the hospital, during the biopsy procedure, where doctors cut open my gum under my nose to reach back where the tumor was located more easily, I began to bleed excessively. It bled profusely enough that a blood transfusion was ordered. However, the hospital did not have enough AB positive blood in stock, so an ambulance was sent. Again, I cannot imagine how frightened my parents must have been. Would this halt the alcohol addiction? It did not.

I was more uncomfortable than I had ever been upon waking. This was nothing like the double hernia repair surgery I had at age nine. I had packing in my nose that blocked that area and then some, tightly. The doctor would come in daily to replace it, and that was extremely painful. On one occasion, I sat up quickly as he pulled the blood-soaked gauze out, and blood shot out in a stream. I was petrified with fear of the pain and of the unknown. I recalled the blessing that stated, "The impurities would flow with the blood."

Before the end of one week, while my mother was visiting in my hospital room, she received a phone call and rushed out noticeably upset. My parents told me in later years that it was my doctor calling with a diagnosis report of my biopsy. A very unprofessional and uncompassionate thing to do to any parent.

The tumor biopsy had been sent to two different army medical specialty posts in the United States. They reported the same finding—osteosarcoma, a type of bone cancer. This type of cancer is usually found in the limbs, which are sometimes amputated to save a life, especially back in the 1960s. My tumor was too advanced for any treatment such as chemotherapy. The medical specialists told my parents they would be fortunate to get me home. I was in the hospital for three weeks.

Years later, my father told me he needed compassionate spiritual guidance after the shock of my diagnosis report and went to a church leader in our ward. This leader heard my father's heart-wrenching story of his oldest daughter facing death any day. His reply was not anything my father had expected or needed. "Well, brother, maybe you should have been attending to your church duties better, and this would not have happened."

My father could feel himself begin to shake but kept his composure. "That is not the God I believe in. He would not punish an innocent child for her father's sins. If that is the kind of God you believe in, you can have him!" This church leader is a flawless example of the statement "The Gospel of Jesus Christ is perfect, but the members are not."

As my parents were contemplating how to tell their daughter at the early age of twelve that she was going to die soon, they decided not to divulge that to me. That was a huge weight on their shoulders though. They confided in some adults in our neighborhood and church. If anyone noticed anything "off" in my appearance or a severe bloody nose, they should call for an ambulance at once. Even though my parents asked to keep this confidential, some told their children. And believe me, I heard about it. "My parents said you're going to die."

I would laugh and say things like, "I feel fairly alive!" The school nurse's office had a memo about me, and a friend saw and reported it to me. The skating rink managers had a memo also, and another friend told me about it.

During these long years, whenever I heard my mother crying behind their closed doors, I thought my parents were having an argument. Now I wonder if any of those times were her fear of losing me. They would never acknowledge it to me the many times I questioned them if I were going to die. I remember as the four of us children got older, oddly, the more often my parents retreated to their *other side*. Was this a need or an excuse to escape reality? I believe it is an addiction, nothing more.

The many evenings that all was "normal," my parents would say as they closed our door in the evening, "Good night. I love you. Sweet dreams." My sister and I then repeated that to each other every night, when we shared a bedroom, before going to sleep. (I have wondered if our brothers said the same to each other.)

I had monthly doctor appointments in San Diego for sinus "inspection." At age fifteen, I asked my doctor, with my mother present, if the tumor was malignant or benign. He was honest, and I was told the truth that I had bone cancer, malignant. This was a relief to me because I was annoyed with people I knew pointing and saying, "Hey, I thought you were dead!"

From recent follow-up x-rays at that time, my doctor told me the tumor had receded from my eyes and sinus area. He could not explain what was going on and had never seen this type of cancer recede. I knew in my heart, even then, that I was blessed with a miracle. My parents did not admit to me the facts, which I already knew until I was eighteen years old and about to get married.

*Do not throw away a man or a woman, old or young. If they
commit an evil today and another tomorrow, but wish to
be Saints and to be forgiven, do you forgive them, not only
seven times, but seventy times seven in a day if their hearts are
fully set to do right. Let us make it a point to pass over their
weaknesses and say, "God bless you in trying to be better in time
to come," and act as wise stewards in the kingdom of God.*[2]

—President Brigham Young

1   https://www.churchofjesuschrist.org/study/manual/gospel-topics/priest-hood-blessing?lang=eng

2   Brigham Young, *Journal of Discourses*, 8:368 https://ldsquotations.com/author/brigham-young/page/2/

# VACATION TWILIGHT ZONES

Our family went on at least two vacations each year, lasting two days to two weeks. The treasured memories I have are of those that went smoothly, uninterrupted by my parent's *other side*. The four of us never knew if that would happen, usually on our way driving home. We came to recognize that it probably would not happen driving back to California from Arizona, where we spent a lot of Christmas and Thanksgiving holidays with relatives. The shorter the drive home, the chances are we would go directly home.

Some of the greatest vacations were at a cabin in Utah that my grandparents owned. My siblings and I share cherished memories of the cabin. There were always cousins there and a lot of exciting outdoor things to do. My mother had spent a lot of time there growing up and was proficient at fly-fishing. I enjoyed fishing and hiking around in the beautiful mountains, even as a teenager.

After the trout were caught, the men scaled and cleaned them up, and the women would fry up some delicious fish. There were always homemade biscuits and gravy to go with the meal. The nostalgia of this memory almost brings the wonderful smell back. I have not been able to match that delectable taste or smell of trout on my own or in any restaurant in all these years since then.

The evenings at the Utah cabin are memorable as well. Many of us would roast marshmallows over the fire in the fireplace. My older relatives would tell stories from the past that were more entertaining than I would have thought. We laughed. A lot! I thought this place was huge as a kid because of all the people that fit inside. But then, visiting with my own family years later, it looked like it had shrunk.

Seems like we always stayed there for about five days. Then came the drive home. Would we make it home in two days after an overnight in a hotel halfway home? As a teenager, that was always the question that plagued my mind. It felt like a twilight zone movie, not knowing if my parents would change to their *other side*. If that happened, we would not make it home for up to another week. My parents always found a hotel with a pool to keep their four children entertained. After one day, however, I was bored. I wanted to go home and talk to friends. And go skating. I doubt all my siblings got bored as fast as I did. I remember Andrew thought it was so cool to get to swim every day.

There always had to be a bedroom with a door that was locked, and my parents would go in and out when the paper bag with the clanking bottles was retrieved from a nearby store. We did not go hungry as they gave us money to buy food.

We also vacationed to places like Idaho and New Mexico, where some of my father's relatives lived, as well as Mexico, Palm Springs, Sequoias, Grand Canyon, and the Salton Sea.

When we stayed with relatives, all was normal and fun. Visiting Idaho, my father and his sister harmonized beautifully, and again, we laughed. A lot.

Most of the time, when our family stayed in a hotel or cabin without relatives, my parents transformed to their *other side*. As the four of us got older, we sometimes voiced our opinions. There were at least two times when I found their stash and began to pour vodka down the drain. My father detested my actions and was upset at all the money wasted. I would tell him it was wasted more when it was poured into their guts. They would usually go buy more.

My friends thought I was lucky to go on long vacations yearly. I never told any of them what else was going on in our twilight zone vacations. Besides, I always hoped that "this" would be the last time they went to their *other side*. They had the potential to be such cool parents.

*What is the remedy? The first thing we must understand is that addictions are so much easier to prevent than to cure. In the Savior's words, "Suffer none of these things to enter into your heart." The best defense against addiction is never to start.*

*But what of those who find themselves in the grip of addiction? Please know, first of all, that there is hope. Seek help from loved ones, Church leaders, and trained counselors. The Church provides addiction recovery help through local Church leaders, the Internet, and in some areas, LDS Family Services.*

*Always remember, with the Savior's help, you can break free from addiction. It may be a long, difficult path, but the Lord will not give up on you. He loves you. Jesus Christ suffered the Atonement to help you change, to free you from the captivity of sin. The most important thing is to keep trying—sometimes it takes several attempts before people find success. So don't give up. Don't lose faith. Keep your heart close to the Lord, and He will give you the power of deliverance. He will make you free.*[1]

—Dieter F. Uchtdorf

1 Elder Dieter F. Uchtdorf, "Are You Sleeping through the Restoration?" LDS General Conference, https://www.churchofjesuschrist.org/media/video/2014-04-0170-president-dieter-f-uchtdorf?lang=eng&alang=eng

# SUICIDE SAVING GRACE

Along with the gal friends I made at the skating rink, I also had boy-friends. Most went to different schools, so we only saw each other on Friday or Saturday nights at the skating rink during the school year. We talked as often as possible from home on those phones with long slinky-like cords attached. Not much privacy there.

Some of Andrew's and my friends rode dirt motorcycles as we did. There were times we would go riding together in the nearby canyons. We would ride along the border of Mexico, which was an over-whelmingly sad sight at times. Some of the children across the small wire-fenced border only had a shirt on and nothing else. I gained an appreciation for my life in the United States and, at the same time, empathy for the unfortunate across the wire fence.

With all the entertainment the four of us had, the few traumatic times seemed to overwhelm me. It is my goal to open the realization to parents nowadays that rough periods can outweigh the greater pleasant times. A parent's example shines in an extreme mode to their children, be it positive or negative. When I had more to deal with in my teenage years besides my parents' *other side*, I became extremely depressed.

One of these depressive states that I recall was when I was sixteen years old, and my boyfriend and I had broken up while at the skating rink. I felt I had hit the solid bottom of an endless pit. I removed my skates, hung them over my shoulder, and went out in the dark to be alone, to cry. The darkness became more intense because of my state of mind.

This rink was situated next to a main busy street. All I could see were headlights. I could seriously be finished with worrying about my parent's *other side*, and had no need to think about a boyfriend hurting me ever again or helping my siblings. After all, I was not supposed to have lived this long anyway.

I stood facing the traffic, trying to push my foot onto the pavement. The images of Andrew, Lisa, and Rick exuded into my mind. I walked a bit further up the sidewalk, attempting to gain the courage to end my despondency. God had my back again, as He did years ago on the street in Phoenix, Arizona. I felt greater compassion for my three siblings that night and knew they needed me to stay.

They had no idea they were my saving grace that evening. No fall, no scrapes, no bandages needed on this occasion. My emotional "boo-boos" were suppressed for a while. I gained what composure I could and went back inside the skating rink until the embarrassing yellow taxicab pulled up to take the four of us home.

*There surely must be someone who yet needs your forgiveness. And please don't ask if that's fair—that the injured should have to bear the burden of forgiveness for the offender. Don't ask if "justice" doesn't demand that it be the other way around. No, whatever you do, don't ask for justice. You and I know that what we plead for is mercy—and that is what we must be willing to give.*[1]

—Jeffrey R. Holland

1   Elder Jeffrey R. Holland, "I Stand All Amazed," Ensign, August 1986, 72 https://abn.
churchofjesuschrist.org/study/ensign/1986/08/i-stand-all-amazed?lang=
eng&adobe_mc_ref=https%3A%2F%2Fwww.churchofjesuschrist.org%2F
study%2Fensign%2F1986%2F08%2Fi-stand-all-amazed%3Flang%3Deng
&adobe_mc_sdid=SDID%3D49398A2A2BD229AD-586CA5D448B-
5154C%7CMCORGID%3D66C5485451E56AAE0A490D45%2540Ado-
beOrg%7CTS%3D1653174860

# EXAMPLE FALLOUT

None of us are perfect, and because of our Savior's Atonement, we can repent daily and continue to progress. It may take years of repenting over and over again to accomplish this in various aspects of our life. And it is not our place to judge anyone on their repentance journey, such as where they are or what they should be doing. It is a private matter between each individual and the Lord.

My sharing of these painful life experiences is to lift burdens and give hope to those suffering in similar situations. I also desire to open the eyes of parents (or others) who are not sincerely setting the best example for their children 24-7. Keep in mind that the many great family times I experienced lessened the happy magnitude with the occasional traumatic situations. I became emotionally damaged. I also was humbled by my situation.

Like most teenagers, I was sometimes tempted to follow the crowd. I was curious why my parents and others would drink until intoxicated. I knew in my heart it was a bad choice. Perhaps it could be fun at the moment, though, just once.

Temptation gave in at one point when a few girlfriends wanted to try a beer or whatever we could get our hands on. They were also members of The Church of Jesus Christ of Latter-day Saints. This one evening, I would be able to drive our family's beat-up station wagon to a drive-in with these friends. I knew where to find alcohol.

While my parents were gone somewhere to their *other side* away from home, I showed one friend where beer was hidden. I told her it was for when they had company who drank. She even believed me! I knew my parents' preferred alcohol was the strong stuff such as vodka, so perhaps they had forgotten about the four six-packs of beer hidden in the garage rafters. But we only took three as not to deplete their stash. I figured they would forget how many they saved anyway.

Five of us teenage girls jumped into the light-green beat-up car that seated six, and off we went to a nearby drive-in theater. We were giggling the whole way, and I was a bit nervous, wondering if we would get caught. Guess I was not nervous enough though. Of course, I have no idea years later which movie we went to "watch."

I remember we all popped open a can fairly soon after the first movie began. We began sipping beer and laughing at how disgusting it tasted. None of us was enjoying the flavor. How could anyone chug this down and more than one twelve-ounce can? I had some spearmint gum in my purse, so we each chewed on a piece as we tried to choke down the beer. One of my friends snorted as she laughed while drinking the beer, and it squirted out of her nostrils! We were ecstatic with laughter, and it was not because we were drunk. From what I remember, none of us were able to even swig down one can of beer.

It was helpful that we were not able to get even close to being intoxicated, especially myself, since I was driving. But after all, I knew my parents drove after drinking. And a lot more than I had planned on! We did chew a lot of gum that evening, and we did laugh ourselves silly. I doubt few of us had any desires to try alcohol ever again. I returned three six-packs of beer to my parents' hiding place in our garage. They never did mention the one missing six-pack of beer.

As a senior in high school, I decided to stay as busy with positive shaping and fun activities as possible. I joined speech, was on our school's Girls Athletic Association, tried out and made the drill team and gymnastic team. My sister, Lisa, was also on the drill team. My parents went to a couple of parades in which the drill team performed. But they never attended any gymnastic meets I competed in, which disappointed me. At least two years later, when Lisa was a senior and captain on a drill team, my mother helped the team during the year.

On most school days, I went back to school for an hour of a drill team or gymnastic practice. I only had four periods each day and decided to job search. If I landed a job and saved money, I would be able to move out upon high school graduation. My parents had never discussed options, including college or jobs, so I was unprepared for the outside world. I never secured a job partly because of my school schedule.

When my father was in his late eighties, I touched on this time period with him. He said that he did remember I was on the gymnastic team. I mentioned to him that it would have meant a lot to me if my parents had attended any of my competitions. He said he was sure they must have, but he does not remember any. One of the greatest moments of being a parent to me was attending my children's many activities. There is no way to count how many or the value those memories have for me. My parents missed out on countless times that would have brought us emotionally closer.

About midway through my last year in high school, I had a serious boyfriend. We related similarities as his family was dysfunctional too. But mine was only part-time, and his was full-on dysfunctional. As my parents occasionally changed to their *other side*, I became overly anxious to move out. Patience in my young heart had vanished. I asked two different close friends to speak to their parents about my moving in. I would do all the chores they asked for and not eat very much. Of course, that was a negative.

Looking back upon my next choice is rather agonizing. My boyfriend and I decided we should attempt to get pregnant. After all, we were in love. And this way, we would have an excuse to move out of our parents' homes by getting married. We could choose because we were eighteen years old, which is a legal adult.

Being young and dumb has drawbacks. Having been taught at church to have strong morals and get married in the temple was implanted in me. But so was the blessing of repentance. It sure would have prevented a lot of hurts to do things the right way the first time. But it seemed like we were both relieved as we made plans. My boyfriend was going to join the air force after earning his GED before he could graduate high school. This was not planned out well at all. How could we move out of our parents' homes without income?

My parents seemed highly disappointed, with my father being mostly angry, when they found out I was pregnant. I was on another spectrum—sick, sick, sick! I never knew that a tiny baby inside you could cause that much greenery! I could not even keep water down most of the time. But my parents seemed mostly concerned about what people would think of them if they found out their daughter in high school was pregnant.

A surprising call one week before our wedding date occurred. The school counselor called me in to discuss something that had landed in my lap (not a baby). San Diego State University had asked the counselors to give the most qualified female student a full-ride four-year physical education scholarship. They chose me, and I cannot say how shocked I was. Looks like God once again had my back, but unfortunately for me, I had made other plans.

I had taken SATs earlier in the year but never applied to any colleges. I had thought about a junior college but did not want to live at home. Turning that scholarship down was a no-brainer. I told her as soon as I got married, my husband would be in basic training and then we would not be living in the area. In my heart, I was wounded, but there was no going back, of course. Having a baby is something I could handle and love. Planning on not being an example fallout was at the top of my list.

My parents spoke with my boyfriend and I, and we confirmed that we were all about getting married. Things were set up ASAP.

My parents called our bishop and arranged a date to perform a ceremony in our home. I was instructed not to mention my little situation to anyone, not even our bishop. They did not want the embarrassment of anyone knowing their daughter was pregnant. I felt bad about all this and did not expect a nice wedding dress or anything else. However, normalcy to the outsiders would appease my parents. We had a pretty "at home" wedding and have the pictures as proof. Our bishop was never told we were going to have a baby in eight months. I wonder if he suspected it.

To my knowledge, being married while in high school was not something anyone at my school had done previously. I reported my last name change to the high school office after I was married. The front desk gals were a bit confused as to how to handle this. My story was that my husband would soon have his GED and had already put in his application for the air force. Only one of my friends knew the main reason I got married.

Because of severe nausea, my attendance in school suffered. By doing all my makeup work, I kept my GPA higher than 3.5. I decided I was not up to the practice and competition that the drill and gymnastic teams required. Teachers must have been perplexed as I ran out of class unexpectedly a couple of times. I had radar on every bathroom for those nauseating moments. This was not at all what I had expected!

At seven months pregnant, I left my parents' home for one and one half months to Rantoul, Illinois, where my husband was in air force school training as an egress man. He would become skilled at installing and repairing ejection seats.

My parents helped me pack two extremely large suitcases, no rolling wheels back then. I had dishes and even a small TV stuffed in my baggage! Porters had to help the pregnant girl.

Living alone and independent was a joy, even as poor as we were. By this time, I was feeling better, always hungry, but had constant heartburn. However, that was a major relief from the first six months.

After our return to Imperial Beach, California, in December, our first baby, a nine-pound boy, was born. Interestingly, I gave birth to my baby at the same hospital that my parents had been given my gloom-o-death report seven years previously. This was a pivotal moment for me. After many hours of labor and forceps help, my infant son entered the brightly lit room and was immediately placed across my stomach. I felt a loving understanding beyond anything I had ever felt. I now understood what an eternal love could be.

For several months before my son's birth, I had been prayerfully persevering to read the entire Book of Mormon for the first time. Until this miraculous moment of witnessing my baby's birth, I had not really felt a confirmation of its wonderful truths. Knowing my parents had an eternal marriage was difficult for me to comprehend. How could anyone desire to be with someone for eternity? I am thankful for my Heavenly Father and my first baby boy for giving me that delightsome taste of honey.

When our son was one month old, the air force stationed my husband in Tucson, Arizona, for eleven months. We were appreciative that my father, having connections with secondhand furniture, helped us with our needs in our two-bedroom apartment close to the air force base. Being away from my parents' home since then gave me relief, but knowing my siblings dealt with the problem occasionally hurt my heart.

While we were in Tucson, an ENT specialist became interested in my previous bone cancer diagnosis as I required monthly appointments. He wanted to perform another biopsy as he believed that I had received an incorrect prognosis. He said that I would not be alive if I truly had osteosarcoma.

I signed for this air force ENT doctor to acquire my records from the hospital in California. My foremost concern was the bleeding complication I had had at age twelve. My doctor assured me they would have AB positive blood available, and I would stay overnight in case of complications.

The surgery was performed through my gums once again, and I did not have any bleeding problems. The biopsy came back within one week. The report was perplexing to my doctor. Yes, there was a large tumor winding back toward the stem of my brain, and evidence that it had receded from my sinus area. It was a large boney mass, a dead mass. It was not diagnosed as anything else.

My doctor asked if I would sign for him to take all my records to a medical convention he was attending soon and told me to make a follow-up appointment in six weeks. I signed permission forms and set up that appointment.

Upon my arrival at my follow-up, the reception seemed confused, saying I had no appointments set up as my doctor had retired during that time. I went to the records department to sign my records out, but there were none there. The doctor had never brought them back. Neither the records department nor I was allowed to call him. This has been problematic for me from 1973 every time I have a change in doctors. My father says he thinks my case with diagnoses and scans lights up a medical book somewhere.

I believe in miracles. Most doctors who take my case somehow believe those two biopsy reports from separate labs were wrong. It saddens me to know they cannot see the truth because they did not live it. I am here, alive and well, knowing that God has had my back.

*Practicing forgiveness can have powerful health benefits.
Observational studies, and even some randomized trials, suggest
that forgiveness is associated with lower levels of depression, anxiety,
and hostility, reduced substance abuse, higher self-esteem, and
greater life satisfaction. Yet, forgiving people is not always easy.*[1]

1 "The Power of Forgiveness," February 12, 2021, https://www.health.harvard.edu/mind-and-mood/the-power-of-forgiveness Mind & Mood

# FATHER'S PERFECT JOB

Around age thirty, my father landed the career that took him into his retirement in his early sixties. He remained operational manager of three thrift stores with signs "Profits for the Retarded" for thirty years. This was about sixty years ago, and thankfully the R-word has been ousted for the most part. This opened my interest in those with special needs in my late teens.

I had gone to work a few times with my father and got to know some of the developmentally delayed youth who had job training there. They really intrigued me with their sense of love for all and had interesting personalities. Caring less about what others thought would be a valuable personality trait they all had. My father's job kick-started my career of working with individuals with special needs for thirty-five years and writing two books about my journey.

Before my father passed away in February 2022, we had a lot of conversations about his life. He told me that his thirty-year occupation was the perfect job for him and our family. He implemented a lot of positive changes when he first took over. The stores quickly picked up business and higher profits. Because he had consistent and trustworthy assistant managers, he was able to take off whenever he wanted.

My parents had more freedom than most who held jobs. I could understand how they could change to the *other side* and come out smelling like roses per se. Be it two days or two weeks, my father still had employment. And his stores stayed on top of the game. He was highly respected and valued in his position. I have no doubt that my father was an intelligent man.

As adults, we had been given the excuse of why we moved so often. It was because others kept finding out that their oldest daughter could die any day, so they would relocate to start afresh for me. Having many school changes was a lot more difficult to swallow than people asking me, "Hey, when are you going to die?" So that explanation of our many moves they provided does not add up.

No matter where we lived, my parents stayed close to each other, and my mother would say she would follow her husband to a city dump if that was where he wanted to go. She was jealous of any woman who would even look at him. This stayed true to course throughout her whole life.

In the last few years of my mother's life, her health was spiraling downward. Eventually, she was placed in an assisted living facility. Every day my father would be at her side. I know if she had been in a dementia state, it would not have detoured him from attending to her needs and loving her completely.

Yes, his career choice was a perfect job for him. But more so, his marriage choice was the perfect job for him, which is for time and all eternity. I can picture my parents up above embracing, dancing, laughing, teaching others, and never changing to their *other side* because of our Savior's Atonement.

*Forgiveness is not erasure. Rather, it's about changing your reaction to those memories.*[1]

—Dr. VanderWeele

[1] Dr. VanderWelee, "The Power of Forgiveness," https://www.health.harvard.edu/mind-and-mood/the-power-of-forgiveness

# DANGEROUS CONSEQUENCES

My parents did not always drink behind closed doors. I am certain we do not know about it all of the time, and I am perfectly fine not knowing anymore. Some extremely dangerous consequences of our parents' drinking that the four of us experienced will be mentioned here.

When I was almost thirteen years of age, I recall my parents had gone out one evening. I woke to my mother crying in the bathroom. What a sight my mother was when I saw her! Her dark black eye makeup was all smeared and running down her cheeks. The scene reminded me of something I had seen in a horror movie. She was shaking and extremely upset, throwing trash out of her purse.

My mother showed me several white tags that had different women's names and phone numbers on them. Someone had planted them in her purse. Each had the same style of writing on them but was not my father's writing. Being the jealous wife she had always been, she knew some lady did this in hopes of getting my father's attention. My mother was frantically ripping each of them up, at least a dozen small pieces of paper. My father was not home yet. She had taken a taxi home. In my young mind, it was really stupid! I recognized that the alcohol was in control of these adults.

Then my mother showed me something more upsetting. She lifted up her skirt and displayed tire track marks across her thigh! I was told that when she left wherever they were (a bar?), someone's car she bumped into did not have a parking brake set, and she fell. The car rolled over her leg and hit the curb. Then I guess the taxi showed up and took her home. (I wonder if she got offered any shrimp?) She could have been killed. I was scared out of my mind. I could not convince her to call an ambulance.

I only went back to bed because my mother told me to. I am sure that was a sleepless night for me. Then in the morning, I got up and went to my junior high school.

After approximately two days of my parents being gone to their *other side* in their bedroom following that awful evening, I returned home from school, as usual, and my mother was her normal cheery self again, except for a severe limp. She had the top of her leg in an Ace bandage which looked professionally wrapped, so I was relieved she had seen a doctor. My father came home from work and was served his freshly cooked dinner. I did not mention the happenings of that night because it was too difficult for me.

I had one boyfriend whose mother said she knew who my parents were as she had seen them in a local bar. They also knew my family were members of The Church of Jesus Christ of Latter-day Saints. I tried to brush it off, telling my friend it could not have been my parents. But then whenever his mother spoke with me, she brought it up. I still recall the smirky smile on her face as she puffed away on her cigarette. She said she still sees my father in that bar now and then. I felt betrayed and embarrassed.

One of my siblings, when older, got a call one evening. (I did not find this out until just a few years ago.) The police had picked up our father for intoxication. My father made his one phone call, and my sibling went to the downtown San Diego Police station's holding tank for those who were brought in for being under the influence.

I am not sure if there was a fight that evening. But I remember my father had been in a fight and broken his nose at one time. This holding tank was full of individuals who appeared to be in a homeless state. The smell was almost nauseating. Looking completely out of place, my father rushed to get out when he saw his grown child picking him up. To say he appeared to be humiliated is an understatement.

I only heard recently about another time that happened while my parents had been drinking, gone to their *other side*. People may surmise that they did this because they enjoyed it. At first, I heard you enjoy it, but things can get out of control. All of these times I recall were certainly not enjoyable for my siblings or for me. By this time, I had already moved out of my parents' home.

In Rick's words:

I think I was about thirteen years of age. Mom and Dad were in their room. At this point, for days. I was on the couch, watching TV, and it was fairly late in the evening, and the streets and neighborhood were quiet, when there was a somewhat forceful knock at the door. Not like a kid but like an adult. I cautiously went to the door and peered through the door window to see four Imperial Beach police officers there. I opened the door, now more curious than scared.

"Hi," one said to me.

"Uh, hi." (Maybe I was in trouble?)

They asked, "Is Anna here?"

I replied, "Uh, well, Anna is here."

They asked, "Can we see her?"

At this point, I was starting to think Mom and Dad were FINALLY in trouble for drinking! I said, "Sure." I proceeded down the dark hallway to their closed bedroom door and knocked and said (loudly), "Mom and Dad, the cops are here to see you!" I hadn't realized that the police officers came into the house and followed me down the hallway. They were right on my heels. I was laughing under my voice, rather elated that they were finally going to "get it!"

One of the police officers asked me to come outside with him, to remove me from the situation. Smart. As I was leaving the house, the police officers continued to tell my parents they needed to come in to get Mom (Anna). I still thought they were just in trouble for being drunks.

The police officer took me out front, where I saw two police cars in front, but their lights were not on. The officer told me to take a seat on the hood of the car. I looked at him and said, "Are you sure?"

He responded with, "Sure, hop on up there!" Now this was highly unusual, especially since these were the days of Levi 501s with rivets on the pockets that would definitely scratch paint, but heck, I took him up on the offer. There he kept my mind on other things, asking me about what sports I liked. At this point, I had absolutely no idea what was going on inside.

A few minutes later, an ambulance arrived with flashing lights but no sirens. Of course, I could now see neighbors peering out their windows at the commotion, but I still didn't understand what was going on. The ambulance workers went inside with a gurney and, after a bit, returned with Mom being followed by the rest of the police contingent. The police officer in charge of me said something nice, shook my hand, and they retreated into the darkness. All was quiet and dark again.

Dad came out around the corner to the car and said that "we" needed to go to the hospital and pick up Mom. I informed him that there was no way I was getting into the car with him driving. He let me know, "No, I'm OKAY now." I'm sure the events had sobered him up quickly, and I hesitantly got into the car with him driving, and we headed to the hospital emergency room.

In the ER, we went in and stood next to Mom, who had a curious-looking dish, banana-shaped, on her chest. I had no idea what this was for but would soon find out as she started vomiting into it. Dad whisked me away to protect her, and me from me witnessing this. I still had no clue what was happening or why.

We left a brief time later, and on the drive home, Dad said, "Well, I'm sure the neighbors are going to be asking questions, so you just tell them that Mom got 'food poisoning.'" Now even though I didn't know what had transpired, I knew "food poisoning" was a lie or why would he say "just tell them." I think he thought I actually knew what had happened or he would have just lied to me by saying, "Boy, your mom really got sick on some Hom's Teapot Inn." But I knew a lie when I heard it.

It was only later when I heard from my grandma and one of my aunts, who were concerned about me being at home when this happened and talked to me. Mom had, in fact, taken a bunch of pills, I think Valium, which I know she had, and then called her mother and one sister to tell them goodbye. They, in turn, called the Imperial Beach Police Department.

Who knows if she took enough to kill her? Who knows if the combination of not enough pills and alcohol would have done the job? I'm not sure we can know.

Looking back on this, I must admit I'm disappointed that THIS wasn't the bottom for them. You'd think that your wife trying to kill herself would be enough to snap you out of it and make you seek help. That, and the fact that they exposed me to this situation, then asked me to lie about it. Unreal that this wasn't enough.

Anyway, that's what happened that night. I gained a great deal of respect for the police, which, in my opinion, handled it in such an amazing way. Of course, I also learned to have much less respect for my parents (until many years later), specifically Dad, and there were certainly more times like this to come.

Rick

*Addiction had the capacity to disconnect the
human will and nullify moral agency.*[1]

—Boyd K. Packer

1   "Revelation in a Changing World," General Conference, October 1989, https://quotefancy.com/quote/1506042/Boyd-K-Packer-Addiction-has-the-capacity-to-disconnect-the-human-will-and-nullify-moral

# PREDICTABLE TIMING

Whenever I returned home from school on a few occasions, my father's car was parked in the driveway, and my heart sunk. He should have still been at work. This could be the start of them going to their *other side*. Their bedroom door locked, smoky smell, bottles clanking—all too familiar forewarnings to their four children.

If the refrigerator became bare, all we had to do was to knock on their door and let them know we needed money for food. From underneath the door, they would slide a ten- or twenty-dollar bill. Yes, that is correct. Yes, my parents invented the first ATM.

There were a few stretches when I was a teenager when my parents would leave the seclusion of their bedroom while I was home. These times were more disturbing than if they had stayed locked away. They would be having a heated discussion, and my mother just wanted to walk away. I cannot describe all the personal details except to say they said things out of character from our sober parents. It is difficult to this day, at age seventy, for me to erase such things from my memory.

After I was married and raising my own family, I began to predict the times when my parents would not be in attendance to certain family gatherings or celebrations. Also, my sister, Lisa and I could tell by our mother's voice over the telephone when they had gone to their *other side*. It was such a disheartening feeling for us. We would suspect, and then we would find out we were correct. Of course, we always hoped that we were wrong. It would make me physically sick to my stomach. I would have no appetite until they returned to being my cool parents. I would lose weight unintentionally.

After four years in the air force, my husband (at the time) and our two small children moved back to California. We eventually had four children before we got divorced. Our third child was born close to Valentine's Day, which was my parents' anniversary. That was always one of the times my parents would change to their *other side.* My parents missed about every birthday celebration of our third child.

With seven years in between the oldest and youngest, Rick got left behind after his three siblings had moved out. The perspective of the oldest, second, third, and fourth child is all different. I felt like a babysitter and caregiver while living with my parents. The caregiving continued past that.

It seems as the four of us discuss our views about growing up that Rick and I got hit the hardest with painful experiences that somewhat damaged us. Yes, our family looked typical from the outside. Here again, parents need to recognize how much the negative moments outweigh the positive times and shape their children's lives.

*Destroy the seed, and the plant will never grow. Man alone, of all creatures of the earth, can change his thought pattern and become the architect of his destiny.*[1]

—President Spencer W. Kimball

[1]  Spencer W. Kimball, "The Miracle of Forgiveness," https://www.goodreads.com/quotes/1278704-destroy-the-seed-and-the-plant-will-never-grow-man

# NOT ALONE

Rick must have felt especially alone with his three older siblings out on their own. At the end of high school, he decided he was going to serve a mission. On his own, he submitted his mission papers to his bishop.

The bishop was taken aback as he spoke with Rick. I imagine the bishop had never interviewed such a spiritually clean youth ready to serve as my youngest brother. And it must have been odd that his parents were not with him or even knew he had turned in his mission papers.

Years earlier, Andrew had served a two-year mission in Mexico. Before that, while in my teens, Lisa and I had questioned our mother as to why our brothers did not have to do any housework or cook meals. Her response was that the boys would learn while on their missions. It did not turn out that way, as my brothers served missions in Mexico and Thailand. Amusingly, both had maids included in their monthly payments on their missions.

Getting called to serve a mission in Thailand, far away from home, must have been perfectly fine with Rick. Our father, for some reason, had shown some frustration when Rick had told him he was going to serve a mission. I am not sure what that was about, but they did not go to the temple with either of my brothers the first time.

At that time, the nearest temple was the Los Angeles Temple, about a three-hour drive depending on the time of day. Andrew told me he was quite nervous about going there alone. He prayed for peace, and the evening before going, he had a revelatory dream about some of the things that would take place inside the temple. He was not nervous and had seen much of what happened in his comforting and miraculous dream.

When Rick went to the same temple the first time, he was not alone as Andrew and his wife went with him. By then I had four children and a husband who rarely would attend the temple. It must have been a deeply disappointing time for my brothers to not have their parents in attendance for their first time in the temple.

The stake president had become aware of my parents' on-again, off-again drinking problem before Rick left for his mission. Unable to bear the burden alone of shielding them any longer, Rick reported to his bishop and then the stake president of how our parents reverted back to their *other side* occasionally since they had been married.

They did not believe him at first but then began to remember times when our parents had been MIA. They called my parents in to confirm, and I heard later from Rick how upset they were with him. My father told me a few times about how much Rick had hurt my mother. What about the hurt to their children?

Their unusual high sense of pride may stem back to being raised in the Depression era. This was true, especially for my father, who had truly little growing up. He was always concerned about what people thought of him and did not want to be looked down upon. It was common for my father in his youth to be made fun of by others for the way he dressed and spoke with a Southern accent. My father was released from his calling, but my mother was not. I never understood that.

I am incredibly grateful for a loving stake president who took my younger brother under his loving care. Rick called him many times for help and advice. One of these times came after my parents dropped Rick (Elder Hall) off at the MTC. I heard how some of the young missionaries were crying and had a tough time telling their parents goodbye. My brother did not have that emotion. He said he felt perfectly fine and was completely ready and eager to preach the Gospel of Jesus Christ.

There he was at the MTC, beginning a new chapter in his life as Elder Hall. He decided to give our parents a call to tell them about the enthusiasm he felt. That was not a call he enjoyed, however. Our parents did not make it home yet. They had stopped in Las Vegas for a bender and were enjoying their *other side.*

Anger filled the young missionary's soul. This was not supposed to happen! He reached out to his stake president back home, who comforted him. He assured the new missionary that he was where he needed to be and would be supported the whole two years. Elder Hall knew he could count on emotional and, if needed, financial support from his ward. This experience made my brother stronger and strengthened his testimony in the Gospel of Jesus Christ.

Ultimately, my parents financially supported both of my brother's missions and a close friend of Andrew's—three full-time missionaries. They gained some bragging rights and were proud of the service these young men gave to the Lord's church.

At least my parents did get their temple recommends and witnessed three of their children's marriage temple sealings. None of these took place on or near Valentine's Day, their anniversary.

I admired my brothers for having served two-year missions. They are partially responsible for my husband, Troy, and I serving a senior couple's mission recently. It was quite rewarding and something I will never regret. We are looking forward to serving more missions.

65

*It is my testimony that many of the deepest regrets of tomorrow can be prevented by following the Savior today. If we have sinned or made mistakes—if we have made choices that we now regret—there is the precious gift of Christ's Atonement, through which we can be forgiven. We cannot go back in time and change the past, but we can repent.[1]*

—Dieter F. Uchtdorf

---

[1] Elder Dieter F. Uchtdorf, "Of Regrets and Resolutions," https://abn. churchofjesuschrist.org/study/general-conference/2012/10/of-re-grets-and-resolutions?lang=eng&adobe_mc_ref=https%3A%2F%2Fwww. churchofjesuschrist.org%2Fstudy%2Fgene ral-conference%2F2012%2F10%-2Fof-regrets-and-resolutions%3Flang%3Deng&adobe_mc_sdid=SDID %3D0600A23D70EA9708-480A9B075112DDB0%7CMCORGID%3D-66C5485451E56AAE0A490D45%2540AdobeOrg%7CTS%3D165 3257531

# GRASP OF THE ADVERSARY

After my third child, my first husband and I had our marriage sealed in the Mesa Temple. My parents attended as well, which gave me hope for them, once again, that they would not return to their *other side*. Once again, that was not to be yet. I felt the peace and beauty of my first experience in the temple that day, but I recall my husband did not seem to grasp that completely. Looking back on what I know now, perhaps he had a guilty conscience. The adversary's grasp can do that to a person if they have not fully repented.

We had one more child and bought our first home as life went on. My husband told me that I needed to get a job after our fourth baby to help pay for the balance due on my piano that he had given me for our anniversary. That seemed odd, but I do not regret my career established because of that gift.

The first job was part-time, supervising in the elementary cafeteria during lunch. Two of my children went there, and it was entertaining to get to know other students.

Then I applied for subbing and worked with children with special needs in that school district. It was a perfect fit for my needs. I would be able to work every day because of the shortage of employees needed for special education, or I could decline if, for some reason, I was not able. There were times I had an ill child at home and would not work that day, at a school at least.

My marriage was a struggle. I felt as if my husband was not being open with me. I sensed that there was an invisible wall between us. But he always assured me that there was nothing wrong. Our family was eternal, and we both had church callings. What could possibly be wrong then?

One day before Thanksgiving in the early 1980s, my husband had just returned from a work field trip of five days out of the area. He sat me down after our four children were in bed and wanted to discuss something with me. We had just purchased our nice four-bedroom home, and I totally missed his underlying need to talk. He had been gone for days, and this would be a wonderful time for us to catch up on *us*.

There I dressed accordingly for a couple who had not been together for some time. But my expectations were not on the same page as my husband's. He immediately started talking before I could "start" anything else. "I have something I need to tell you. I have never really loved you. And I know you will want to divorce me now because I want to drink."

Yes, just like that. I am sure the look on my face would have stopped a full-speed-ahead train. "What? We have been together for over ten years, have four beautiful children, and our love is sealed in a holy temple of God for time and all eternity! What is really wrong?"

I was assured that he had thought this through and knew I would want to divorce him because of the alcohol desire. I told him that I would not divorce him for "that" reason. If that was his choice to drink, then so be it. But he could not have alcohol in our home or drink around our children. I would not put them through the things I had been through.

Being completely stunned at my answer, he replied, "You won't divorce me if I want to drink?" I affirmed that was the case. If, however, there are other reasons, he should tell me.

The only other thing he wanted was to be excommunicated from the church. I asked him, "Why, for drinking?" He said that he did not believe it was true and did not want to be a member anymore. I instructed him that he should call our bishop and make an appointment to discuss it. And I cried.

My heart was shattered that evening! I felt numb and devasted. He might as well have stabbed me in the heart as it felt the same. I am sure that sleep did not come to me that night. And then, on Thanksgiving, the next day, all of my family came to our home.

First, I had to cook the meal as I was fighting back Niagara Falls' tears. And even more difficult, choke food down as my parents, sister, and her family joined us in the feast. This was a real nightmare during the daytime.

My sister and I went outside with my children afterward while my husband and her husband offered to clean up. I believe the rest of them watched sports on the TV. Her sweet comment broke the floodgates, "Aren't we lucky to have such nice husbands who want to help us?"

My voice quivered as I gave her the update, "Mine wants a divorce."

I shared the depressing news with her and later with my parents over the phone. We did not compare the wanting to drink similarities. My father was extremely upset and told me if he divorces me, he will divorce the whole family. I was feeling this was more than just about him wanting to drink.

Since the burden of filing for divorce was placed on my shoulders, he agreed that we could try and work on our marriage before doing that. I attempted to get closer to him, sitting next to him more often, even in the car. I even went to one bar with him only because there was dancing. He assumed I would relent and drink with him. Wrong.

Upon leaving that one evening of dancing where he drank and I did not, he stated, "Yeah, you were right. Nothing was different with you."

And I was thinking, *Duh, get thee behind me, Satan*. The adversary's grasp did not relax on my first husband, however.

During this period, we did not tell our children what was going on. I would make excuses that their father had to work late. I carried on, trying to be *normal* for my children, playing with them, helping them, and attending to all of their needs, loving them. And forcing a smile.

I took them to church alone. Sitting in sacrament meeting was testing with my four little ones, ages one to six years old. Then hearing Relief Society[1] lessons about how your spouse should be your best friend. (Gag me.) There were times I could not hold the tears back and hid in a bathroom stall.

We had an anniversary coming up five months after my gloom-and-doom Thanksgiving surprise notice. We decided to book a hotel in the mountains and go horseback riding and hiking. These were all my ideas, but he went along with them. I also had to arrange care for our children.

Not only had he been away from me at intervals during these past few months but he rarely saw our children. Most of the time, after he went drinking, he would spend the night at his mother's house. She was single again after four failed marriages.

Driving up to our planned vacation getaway, he was boasting about his fun time out with his cousin drinking a few days ago. I asked him seriously, "Why can't people just be happy with who they are? Why do they want to be someone they aren't?"

He caught me off guard with his quick retort. "Well, Trixie, not everyone can be perfect like you!" I knew at that moment that this trip was off to a not-so-good start and would continue.

We were eating in a nice little restaurant that evening, and there was dancing—my thing. He refused to dance as I was thinking, *This marriage is really failing.* He must have been thinking that he had already relented to dancing once before, and it did not change my behavior, so what was the use?

Ever since we married at age eighteen, my first husband had been a smoker off and on. Now he could smoke and not have to hide it from anyone. I am not sure if he had quit for a time, even to go to the temple. I seem to be allergic to smoke, and when pregnant, it would cause me to throw up. At least he was considerate enough to smoke outside.

Horseback riding the next day was amusing. I enjoyed it! The one time my husband got off his horse and did not hold the reins like I had warned him to, the horse took off back to the stalls. I knew that is what a smart animal would do if their passenger gave them the opportunity. But my husband did not believe me. Then he expected me to get off of my horse and walk back. That did not happen. He did not walk back. He stomped back, puffing on a cigarette.

This anniversary was a flop in one way and an eye-opener in another. I was losing love and respect for a man I had wanted to be with, as trying as it was sometimes, forever. I had thought if we both worked at this marriage to become the best of friends, we would benefit from it, and our four children would learn from our example to never give up.

Around this time, I had a dream about a man two nights in a row. I was so happy that when I awoke, I had tears on my pillow. This was someone I had known in my childhood and barely saw now and then at church. He was married and had two cute little daughters. He did not look happy though.

In the first night's dream, I was sitting in a dark room next to a man with dark-blond hair. We were holding hands, looking at the fireplace. This man was not my current absent husband because he was shorter. I felt comfortable and in love with him. I never saw his face in that dream, but I sure was happy! The sad part was when I awoke, realizing it was not real.

The next night, I found myself in the same position in my dream. This time the same dark-blond man sitting lovingly next to me stood up. He then got down on one knee and looked up at me, deep into my eyes. He asked, "Trixie, will you marry me?"

I recognized him right away. It was Troy Neal! That part woke me up. This was someone I had known in my youth. He used to write me love notes when I was in seventh grade, and he was in eighth grade. He was extremely shy back then and would have his friend hand me the notes. I would open the notes and see who they were from and proceed to tear them up. This guy was a band nerd! (hindsight).

That morning I called my father and my sister and told them about my dreams. We all had a good laugh as they knew Troy. They asked what I thought it meant and why I would dream about Troy Neal. I did not know why! I never spoke to him, but he dropped off his spunky little girl on Sundays in the nursery. She would run into my arms at once and not let me put her down. Still, I knew the reason at that time for a dream with that extent of happiness was meant for me to know that someday I would be happy again. Hope was alive.

Another two years came and went, and things were not improving. Even though we were still married, I lived like a single parent. I prayed more during this time than probably most times in my life.

This was pure torture, not knowing what the outcome would be. There I went again, losing weight. I had zero appetite. I felt suicidal at one point. I was suffering but could not give in to that. My children were my saving grace this time. I was sealed to them for time and all eternity if I remained worthy. And besides, who could I trust to care for them if I ended my life?

One evening while I pled with my Heavenly Father once again for help and answers, I had the answer. He placed the confirmation in my mind and broken heart that I would be fine. My children would be fine as well. It was time to file for divorce. This relief lifted my spirits immensely. Yet I had no idea how all of this would play out. I just knew without any doubt that it was all going to work out.

When I told my husband I had filed for divorce, he was visibly shaken and surprised. He was enjoying his partying lifestyle and having-your-cake-and-eating-it-too relationship.

He would call me daily to try to coerce me into changing my mind, to no avail. I knew deep within my heart I was doing the right thing.

One thing that flabbergasted me was he actually went to see our bishop on his own and had a church disciplinary council set up. I had figured he would just let that idea go. His being excommunicated was in the works. He mentioned to me how he had done that because he thought it was best since he no longer had a testimony.

By this time, the love I had felt for my husband was completely absent. There were other misbehaviors that warranted his membership records being removed from the church. I had gone through a grieving process. The person I once had loved seemed dead to me.

I remember quite vividly an extremely hot and muggy September day into the evening a few days later. I already had possession of all of our house keys, and my almost ex-husband was living at his mother's house.

That Saturday afternoon, because our home did not have air-conditioning, after my father handed me some cash, I took my children to a movie. And there the air-conditioning was broken down. What a miserable day it had been already!

I could not have imagined how much worse things would get. I kept the bedroom window open to try to get air in. My children were in bed and had the two little fans we owned in their bedrooms. All of a sudden, right at my window came the thundering, loud voice of my husband, "Trixie, we need to talk. Ya gotta let me come in, please."

I gave in because I did not want any disturbance and to give our children bad memories. I let him in the front door, me standing in my nightgown. His breath could have wilted a bed of flowers. Alcohol. I had never witnessed him being this drunk before.

I kept asking him to leave so we could continue our discussion the next day. He was pleading with me to change my mind and not go through with the divorce. I reminded him that we were over as a couple but needed to get along for the children's sake and well-being. This only made him angrier.

I was about to call someone to come help, but he grabbed the princess cordless phone out of my hand and threw it at the glass china hutch door. Crash! Glass shattered and hit the floor along with the phone.

I was beginning to hyperventilate as he attempted to next throw me out of the front door. I held on to the inside doorknob as tight as I could. Even him being twice as large and stronger than me could not remove my hand. He was closing the door as my aching left hand held on to the inside knob. I thought my wrist might break when he finally let go. I fell inside the house and was about to pass out.

"Ah, come on, Trixie. Quit playing around!" he said. I was honestly overwhelmed, and once he realized that I was not faking it, he took off out of the front door to who knows where. He was in his socks. I had not even noticed that he walked in with no shoes.

The neighbors were not located near us as we were on a corner lot downhill from the nearest house. If I called my father, he might come over with his gun. Bad idea. I called the police (911), and it took them a good fifteen minutes to arrive. Apparently, they were having a busy evening. I was hoping my children had all slept through the ruckus with the fans making noise in their bedrooms.

I showed the police the shattered glass and told them of the traumatic experience I had gone through. They asked if he hurt me. I answered that it hurt having my wrist being pushed on by him trying to close the door while shoving me outside. However, I had no visible marks.

They asked who owned the house. We were both still the homeowners but were going to sell it soon. The police said that they could not legally do anything until he had hurt or threatened our children or me since the home was in both of our names.

This was quite frightening to me! I had no idea where he had run off to and what would happen if and when he returned. The police made their report and left, wishing me the best.

Not long after the police left, my missing intoxicated husband returned. He had calmed down, but I still could not get him to leave. Because I wanted to shield my children from their unstable father, I did as he asked and laid down on the bed with him. He was snoring pretty quickly, and it was nearing 4:00 a.m.

As I laid there, praying for guidance, I knew I wanted to leave the house as soon as possible. The first thing I did when I snuck out of bed was to soak in the bathtub in the opposite bathroom down the hall. That helped eliminate some of my anxiety of the exciting events thus far.

Since it was Sunday, I put on my church clothes and quietly began gathering things such as my divorce documents and notes from my attorney. It was not an easy thing to do as I began waking up my children, the oldest first.

I made it seem like an adventure to them to be quiet, so we do not wake their father, and told them we were going to visit their grandparents before going to church. Of course, they were curious as to why their father was there at all.

I was more than relieved when the five of us were ready, dressed in our Sunday best, and heading out to our car in the garage. Opening the garage, I was astounded when I saw his car parked right behind mine in the driveway! Since our garage was detached from the house where our backyard was fenced, I did not see it until the garage door was opened. I almost felt defeated, but I am a stubborn person. His car was locked, and no sign of keys in it. Telling my children to wait while I fetched his car keys, I prayed they were in plain sight.

Again, being extremely quiet, I went back inside, searching for his keys. They were nowhere to be seen. I crept into my bedroom where he laid snoring. The keys were most likely in his pocket, and I was not going to chance to go near him.

At this time, the Internet had not been invented; thus, no social media or cell phones where I could reach out to someone for support. I doubt I would have though, as I tend to be a private and independent person. It is not easy for me to ask for help either. I leaned into prayer that evening.

Then a solution came to me as I walked back out to our garage. Since he was a skilled bike rider, I instructed my oldest son to go to his grandparents' apartment and have Grandpa come pick us up. I knew they were home, but they were not answering their phone. They lived about half a mile from us. My son was my hero that day as I watched him ride off into the sunrise to fetch us a ride.

It did not take long at all for my father to arrive with a quizzical expression on his face. He sensed something was seriously wrong, but we waited to discuss the situation until my children were busy shoveling cold cereal into their mouths. I felt blessed that my parents had not been at their *other side* that morning!

I began retelling my scary few hours tale of the hot night. My father was visibly upset and asked why I did not call him immediately instead of the police first. I told him that I wanted things done legally. After all, my father did own guns. Agreeing with me, he said that he honestly could not promise he would not have lost his cool.

I had him take us by my home on the way to church. My husband's car was gone, and I breathed a long sigh of relief. My children and I were able to commute to church in our own car. I was totally exhausted after the constant adrenaline flow; my main mission of the day was to speak to my bishop.

As the norm for me for the past almost three years, I went into the chapel as a single parent with my four little ones. They were typical children—active, inquisitive, and a bit irreverent in sacrament meetings. As I sat to feel the spirit, I was practically in tears. I gazed around and saw a young woman get up and sit with a couple who had two rambunctious little children to help them. Another elderly sister went and sat with another couple to help with their three children. Was I invisible with my four sweet young overactive children?

If I could go back in time and speak with my younger self, I would give the advice to humble myself and ask for help. I know if I had done that, anyone would have been glad to help me with my children.

Many may question why I put myself through this challenge week after week. I had reread my patriarchal blessing[2] many times as my marriage was in turmoil. Since my parents were told that I would die any day when I was twelve years old, they would not allow me whenever I asked about receiving my blessing. Years later, my mother told me they were afraid I would not have a blessing since my time on earth would not be much longer. They must have been scared and confused about the point of patriarchal blessings.

I initiated my blessing at age twenty-one, as a mother of two (son and daughter). One sentence of my patriarchal blessing kept ringing in my head, especially when I was going through a divorce after four children. "Continue to take your children to church and they will grow into fine young MEN and WOMEN." When I first had that blessing pronounced upon me, I almost laughed and thought that two is enough. Thank you! The Lord is much wiser than I.

Making sure my children were in their classes after an especially long (it seemed) sacrament meeting, I waited by the bishop's door to see if he had time to speak with me. There were about four people ahead of me waiting to see him. Upon opening his door to let one couple out, he looked directly at me and told me to come in.

This man of God was in tune with the spirit for which I have always been grateful. He had counseled my husband and me during the past three years. He recognized that Satan was probably shouting for joy, having claimed another priesthood brethren.

Immediately, as I began relating my experience of the past several hours, I could not hold back the flow of tears. My bishop walked me through the process of how to obtain a restraining order. I did not know that would be allowed as the police did not do anything since we both owned the house. I thanked my bishop, and he ensured the ward was there for me if I ever needed any aid, including groceries.

Once I told my almost ex-husband about the restraining order, he was not happy, of course. But he did honor it. We sold that beautiful home shortly afterward and paid our attorneys with the profit. I moved into a smaller rental home where my children and I no longer had to walk on eggshells. My divorce took a few months because he felt the need to drag things through the court system, nitpicking things such as who would get *my* piano.

I have always wondered if my ex-husband's genetics played any part in his life. His biological father was an alcoholic and physically abusive to his family. After that divorce, his mother married a man who adopted and supported the four children. The biological father never contacted or saw his children again. His mother was divorced and married three more times. My ex-husband had said to me several times, and even upon our divorce, "I will never do to my children what my father did to me." But that is exactly what he did.

Years later, after I was remarried and had a larger family, I wrote a thank-you letter to the bishop who never ignored my problems, elaborating on how much I appreciated his guidance and support. An inspired teacher in Relief Society suggested it to the class. After this past bishop passed away, his wife told me that my letter was one of his valued possessions kept in his journal. I have tried to write handwritten gratitude cards more often after hearing how special it was to one of my bishops.

*Often, we know we need to forgive but we feel overwhelmed by the task and aren't ready to let go of the hurt. We must work at our own pace and recognize that healing may come slowly.*[1]

—Elizabeth Lloyd Lund

1  https://en.wikipedia.org/wiki/Relief_Society

2  https://www.churchofjesuschrist.org/study/manual/gos        pel-topics/patriar-chal-blessings?lang=eng

3  Elizabeth Lloyd Lund, LDS Living, https://abn.churchofjesuschrist.org/study/ensign/2018/04/young-adults/forgiving-others-misconceptions-and-tips?lang=eng&adobe_mc_ref=https%3A%2F%2Fw ww.churchofjesuschrist.org%2Fstudy%2Fensign%2F  2018%2F04%2Fyoung-adults%2Fforgiving-others-misconcep tions-and-tips%3Flang%3Deng&adobe_mc_sdid=SDID%3D498 8AAA548C5E75D-435900C6B138BE4D%7CMCORGID%3D66C548545 1E56AAE0A490D45%2540AdobeOrg%7CTS%3D165 3253809

# HURTFUL TATTLE

After four children and thirteen years of marriage, I was divorced. My ex-husband had seen my parents on their *other side* as I sometimes helped clean up their home afterward. We had decided this was something we would not share with our children in hopes that my parents would someday stop. Our four children were only ages two to ten years of age at the time of our divorce. And sadly, my children's father was drinking quite heavily and eventually lost his employment.

Upon my children being returned after a brief visit (one of few) with their father, the two oldest were noticeably upset and crying. He had told them that their grandmother and grandfather were drunks. I was absolutely crushed that my ex-husband would stoop so low as to hurt our children in this manner. He had told them things he had seen that young children should not have to hear.

Taking my children into a separate bedroom for privacy, I looked them in the eye and explained that sometimes their grandparents did drink alcohol. It was not very often, and they tried to keep it private. My children were still quite shocked. They loved and respected their grandparents. Their father should not have involved them in this spiteful situation. We also discussed why alcohol is harmful to an individual and those they love. That is why the Lord has given us a directive called the Word of Wisdom.[1] As humans, we are not perfect, and the best thing to do is never have that first drink. I had tears in my eyes seeing my children with the disappointment and sadness of the tattling incident from a parent who should have had their best interests at heart. To note, he quit paying child support before we had been divorced for one year.

*Let us not demean or belittle. Rather let us be compassionate. We must be careful that we do not destroy one another's confidence through careless words or opinions… Blame keeps wounds open; only forgiveness heals.*[2]

—President Thomas S. Monson

1   https://www.churchofjesuschrist.org/study/manual/true-to-the-faith/word-of-wisdom?lang=eng

2   https://www.pinterest.com/pin/blame-keeps-wounds-open-only-forgiveness-heals-president-thomas-s-monson-lds-quote--256845984978402326/

# MEETING DREAM MAN

The realistic but not logical dream I had over two years ago, at this time, was stuck in my subconscious. Going through a divorce was miserable. I became the 90 percent statistic of those who marry in their teens being divorced. But I absolutely knew that I was going to be happy again.

The fact that this dream was about someone I had not spoken to since junior high was a bit perplexing. As soon as he would pick up his spunky little girl from the church nursery, she would run right to him. "Daddy!" I wondered if he noticed me always holding her.

Two months after my traumatic evening with my soon-to-be ex-husband, one of my sons was invited to a birthday party by my dream man's sister-in-law. She had a daughter in my son's primary class. That got my curiosity up! Arriving at the birthday party, I spotted a VW Bug with a bumper sticker that said "Ex-wife for Sale. Take over payments." I giggled to myself, thinking that must be his vehicle!

I could have just dropped off my son but decided to scope things out. His sister-in-law introduced us. I found out later she was hoping to get him married so he could move out of their guesthouse in the back. "Oh!" he exclaimed. "I know you!" His sister-in-law had told him about me and that I was also going through a divorce but had four children. He only knew me by my maiden name. Four children did not frighten him away.

I was sizing up this guy who I remembered being the band nerd in junior high. He had matured rather nicely but looked a bit scraggy compared to being in a suit at church.

I was introduced to his two adorable daughters, and, of course, as soon as she spotted me, the younger one jumped into my arms. He had seen that happen but just figured I was doing my job.

I felt hope there. I began to get some appetite back right then and there and enjoyed some delicious chocolate cake. Just to meet a nice guy who listened to me and was interested was different. I knew if we did work out, I could get him to change out of his outdated bell bottoms. That was all unimportant anyway.

This was the beginning of many long conversations, getting to know each other. We did not date but had many outings with either six or four of our children. They made great chaperones. I had full-time custody, and he had part-time. This man was so patient, and he had the best sense of humor. What an insight I felt, recognizing there are nice men out there.

My parents were hoping for this to work. My father told me years later that they knew I was going to have to move in with them with my four children. If they had told me that back then, I would have dropped that idea with a flat "never" to them. I would never live with their *other side* again, even if I had to be homeless. Having my ex-husband drinking excessively was difficult enough for my children to see.

I never mentioned my dream from years ago to Dream Man. I did not want to jinx it! Then one evening after a late afternoon of swimming where he lived, my children piled into my station wagon. Troy was telling me good night outside of my car and suddenly dropped down on one knee on the asphalt in the dark. He gazed up into my eyes. "Trixie, will you marry me?"

I stared at him in disbelief as he continued to look at me, waiting for an answer. I told him under my breath, "That was weird!" He asked me what was weird.

I almost had tears in my eyes and said, "That was my dream from over two years ago!" Of course, he was pretty stoked because he had not planned to do this. The spirit prompted him strongly.

He asked, "Well?" I told him yes and then about my dream. Neither of us had any thought of a ring! That came much later.

It took us nine months from the birthday party meeting to getting married. There was a lot to figure out and to get done. Our incredible bishop counseled us during that time and then married us in our chapel. I was awaiting my temple divorce to be final from my ex-husband before we could be sealed (married) in the Los Angeles Temple for time and all eternity.

My mother made such pretty dresses for our four daughters. All of our children were in our wedding party, including my oldest son, who was the best man and my oldest daughter the maid of honor. They all seemed pretty jazzed.

To say we were excited to leave the wedding party is an understatement. This would finally be our very first date, alone finally. My oldest son had to throw a handful of rice in the car (instead of to the birds) at us as we were leaving. "Ouch!"

My parents gave us a paid weekend at a beautiful hotel overlooking the bay. My brother and his wife stayed with my four children that weekend. Such an epic honeymoon, and first date for us newlyweds.

When our first baby was two months old, almost two years later, I was sealed to Troy, my Dream Man, for time and all eternity in the Los Angeles Temple.

Most of his family came to witness the grand event. My parents were absent because this was their anniversary on February 14, Valentine's Day. They had gone to their *other side* as was their custom on that date. We had a few members there from our ward as well, and everyone was curious as to why my parents were not in attendance. All I could say was, "It's their anniversary today."

Less than three years later, my ex-husband (father of four of my children) passed away at the age of thirty-six from liver cirrhosis. He had only been drinking for about six years.

The last time he visited his four children was a few weeks after Troy and I had our first baby. It was two months after the birthday of my youngest daughter from my first marriage.

Walking in, he tossed the birthday girl an unwrapped toy, barely acknowledging her. Then he asked me if he could hold my baby. I was a bit nervous but figured it should be fine. Holding his ex-wife's newborn baby from another man, he told me how beautiful she was. Then he left. None of us spoke with him or saw him ever again.

I had tried quite a few times to encourage my first four children to contact their father. I would buy a birthday card or Father's Day card and have them sign it. Then I would mail it. No response, and he lived only twenty minutes away from us. He did not even call them. It broke my heart.

One day my two oldest were frustrated with the pretense and asked me why they had to keep sending their father something when he did not even care about them. They did not want to do this anymore. They were mid-teens, so I agreed to let them stop. I told them that they were old enough to make that choice but that their father was sure missing out. And my heart hurt for my children.

After holding my newborn baby, my ex-husband ignored our four children for over three years prior to his death. This left some of our children in a state of limbo, not knowing where they stood with him. There were repercussions because of this for years. At the time of his death, Troy and I had two babies of our own.

And it does not end there with the devastation that alcohol caused in our families. Four years later, Troy's ex-wife, while driving intoxicated, was killed in an auto accident at age thirty-five. This is how my stepdaughters came to live with us permanently. It is not how we expected our prayers to be answered.

Between my four children and his two from our previous marriages, there were emotional scars from losing a biological parent due to alcohol. We spent a lot of time in counseling sessions with our six children and a lot of time on our knees, praying for guidance. Alcohol can lead to pain for years to come. Nobody can predict if they will have self-control upon taking that first drink. Is it worth the chance?

Years after my ex-husband's death, I was speaking to my oldest son, apologizing for his father, who missed so much of life, including several grandchildren. My son told me it is fine because he believes his father was just going through a rough phase. And he feels if he were alive, he would have changed and that all is forgiven. Made me a proud mother for sure.

Today, almost forty years of marriage, Troy and I are closer and more in love. Making the Lord the center of our relationship is key. The appreciation we have for each other is astounding. We feel that in part is due to having first rough marriages.

Of course, it is not always easy at times, especially while raising a large family. Our important beginning was becoming best friends before marrying and being intimate. This built trust in each other and gave us strength in our union. Now it is a forever deal.

*The family is ordained of God. Marriage between man and woman is essential to His eternal plan.*[1]

# Notes

1 "The Family: A Proclamation to the World," https://abn.churchofjesuschrist.org/study/scriptures/the-family-a-proclamation-to-the-world/the-family-a-proclamation-to-the-world?lang=eng&adobe_mc_ref=https%3A%2F%2Fwww.churchofjesuschrist.org%2Fstudy%2Fscriptures%2Fthe-family-a-proclamation-to-the-world%2Fthe-family-a-proclamation-to-the-world%3Flang%3Deng&adobe_mc_sdid=SDID%3D02418F48CF77E098-573922D1E90FF199%7CMCORGID%3D66C5485451E56AAE0A490D45%2540AdobeOrg%7CTS%3D1653253342

# FUN WITH GRANDPARENTS

After letting my parents know that some of their grandchildren now knew their secret, they were extremely saddened that their ex-son-in-law would be so vindictive. After all, he had been a valued member of our family for over ten years. He and my father were buddies and discussed football together, getting along like a father and son. The tie was severed. My ex-husband had not expected that.

My parents owned a thirty-six-foot cabin cruiser, "Cathy-Lou," docked in the marina, and many treasured memories were made there. My older son had a blast fishing with his grandfather and his stepfather Troy. That is probably where he caught his first fish.

On the Fourth of July, all the nearby family would celebrate on the Cathy-Lou, grilling burgers and hot dogs with all the fixings. This included my mother's killer homemade ice cream. When fireworks were displayed, we were directly underneath the beautiful array of fiery colors and some ashes as they gently floated down above the bay.

During these years, most holidays were celebrated at my parents' home, wherever they were living at that time. They became apartment managers in three different condominiums or apartments upon three separate moves.

My father still managed the thrift stores as well. By now my brother Andrew had served a church mission and was married. (Lisa and then Rick got married later.)

In the meantime, while the rest of us lived our own lives and had less interaction with my parents during those tough times, my brother Rick still lived at home, feeling isolated when my parents reverted to their *other side*. Or, as he called it, finding them in a drunken stupor. Rick had a girlfriend whose parents were so kind as to let him sleep over on their living room couch now and then. They did not ask or were told what was going on with Rick's parents but had trusting and compassionate hearts. To this day, Rick is thankful for their caring attitude.

After my family had moved from Florida (air force assignment) back to California, before Rick left for his mission, he lived in our garage. His bedroom was all set up there, and he had privacy. He leaned into playing his guitar at that time. My oldest son enjoyed going jogging with his uncle. I am grateful that my younger brother took time to play with my children.

By this time, I had four children and recognized my marriage was hanging on by a thread. The more time my husband took off with any excuse from keeping the Sabbath Day holy, such as attending church meetings, the further our relationship was teetering. This is what I recall most about those years. Rick was easy to have around, so those memories are not as clear.

My parents are fortunate (and vice versa) that their grandchildren and great-grandchildren have only special recollections of them. It melts my heart with gratitude that treasured memories fill their hearts and that there is no emotional baggage. I admit I feel envious but happy for them. The joy of repentance and forgiveness cannot be measured. "Oh, it is wonderful."

*We have a strange illusion that mere time cancels sin. I have heard others, and I myself recounting cruelties and falsehoods committed in boyhood as if they were no concern of the present speakers, and even with laughter. But mere time does nothing either to the fact or to the guilt of sin. The guilt is washed out not by time but by repentance and the blood of Christ.*[1]

—C. S. Lewis

[1] C. S. Lewis, "The Problem of Pain," https://www.goodreads.com/
quotes/750071-we-have-a-strange-illusion-that-mere-time-cancels-sin

# TAG TEAM

As time went on, more adult family members stepped up to help my parents out when they would flip to their *other side*. It seemed some of these incidents lasted longer, which could be life-threatening. One time, a couple in our family was trying to help by offering food to my parents. My father was upright one second, and the next passed out, hitting the carpeted floor. His tongue had gone backward down his throat. They immediately called 911 and then started CPR. It was such a godsend that my brother-in-law had a medical background, knew how to respond, and stayed calm.

My father spent one week in the hospital stabilizing his electrolytes. I spent a few days that week cleaning their home and assisting my mother with her health as she spent time visiting her husband in the hospital. The usual things I did were to clean out their refrigerator, clean the bathrooms, do laundry, vacuum, and mop. This usually facilitated my losing weight once again, which I was not looking to do. It was extremely stressful by this time as I had a large family and worked in a classroom during school hours. I would have rather been home cleaning my own house but mostly to spend quality time with my children and husband.

My mother became irritated with me at one point this time. She could not find a small bathroom throw rug that she had recently bought. I gave my best effort to explain to her why I had to throw it away. She insisted she could have washed it. But it was too late for that, and I was proud of myself for not using any swear words (which was tempting). I know they were highly embarrassed many times, but I kept up the hope that this would be the final time. Repentance and forgiveness can be and should be a lifelong process.

I was blessed with an understanding and laid-back husband (the second time around) and, to this day, acknowledge I am not sure if I deserve him. My parents said many times that I was truly fortunate. I would jokingly tell my father he must love my husband more than he loved me, his own daughter.

Between the rough spots of helping my parents, we had some special family occasions in their home, such as Thanksgiving and Christmas. My mother would prepare most of the food and loved using her most precious china to serve us. Our children were between the ages of newborn and seventeen years of age by this time, totaling eight. All of my siblings had children as well, so that was an amusing crowd with lots of laughter. These occasions seemed surreal to me, as I knew any day my parents could change to their *other side*. Again, the good times seemed somewhat fake. Nonetheless, I did appreciate them.

Years ago, there was one of those not-so-fun rescue visits we needed to do for my parents. Our children were never told of this. We probably lied and said we or one of us had a meeting or appointment. They certainly did not need that information overload in their young lives.

My husband, Troy, had replaced me at my parents' after he got off work which was later than mine. He caught my father coming out the front door with an extra set of keys in hand. We always confiscated car keys, and we had not found these.

Troy asked him where he was going and said he would drive. My father said he needed something at the nearby convenience store.

Entering the store behind my father, Troy watched as his intoxicated father-in-law stood gazing at the alcohol aisle. Then glancing at Troy over his shoulder, he shrugged, went to the soda display, and picked up a six-pack of Diet Coke.

Tag, you're it! Later, another brother-in-law came to replace Troy, and as he was walking up to the front door, he spotted my father clumsily attempting to maneuver over the backyard wall. His short legs were sprawled over the concrete and slowly coming down the other side. The brother-in-law inadvertently startled him and asked, "So where are we going?" My father had his wallet with him and said he needed to go on a short walk for some fresh air. They went back inside the house.

I never thought babysitting my parents had been a part of my job description as their daughter. But now after all these years and so much has changed, we all just have to laugh at some of these memories. Yes, there are scars, but one must have humor in life!

*Parents have a sacred duty to rear their children in love and righteousness, to provide for their physical and spiritual needs, and to teach them to love and serve one another... By divine design, fathers are to preside over their families in love and righteousness and are responsible to provide the necessities of life and protection for their families. Mothers are primarily responsible for the nurture of their children. In these sacred obligations, fathers and mothers are obligated to help one another as equal partners. Disability, death, or other circumstances may necessitate individual adaptation. Extended family should lend support when needed.[1]*

—The Family: A Proclamation to the World

1    "The Family: A Proclamation to the World," https://abn.churchofje-suschrist.org/study/scriptures/the-family-a-proclamation-to-the-world/the-family-a-proclamation-to-the-world?lang=eng&adobe_mc_ref=https%3A%2F%2Fwww.churchofjesuschrist.org%2Fstudy%2Fscriptures%2Fthe-family-a-proclamation-to-the-world%2Fthe-family-a-proclamation-to-the-world%3Flang%3Deng&adobe_mc_sdid=SDID%3D02418F48CF77E098-573922D1E90FF199%7CMCORGID%3D66C5485451E56AAE0A490D45%2540AdobeOrg%7CTS%3D1653253342

# A CLEAN SLATE

Having two sons who were talented architects was quite an advantage for my parents as my father went into retirement in his early sixties. They sold their boat (ouch) and searched for property in the beautiful mountains of Lake Arrowhead, California.

I remember once the property was found and plans were made to start building, there were a lot of holdups. My parents would go "up the hill," as they called it, and stay in a rented cabin on the weekends to check on progress. We received many step-by-step pictures of their dream home beginnings. Many. I had never seen my parents so frustrated yet excited at the same time.

This home was beautiful, set on a mountaintop, large inlaid brick fireplace, three bedrooms with a loft, a wide driveway with room for two cars, and a boat on a trailer. Yes, my father bought a smaller boat and would pull skiers.

There was a pivotal moment between then and my father being called to serve on the stake high council in Lake Arrowhead. Their children do not know how or when they made this final leap of repentance, but it surely happened. I am guessing the forty years of changing to their *other side* suddenly became a thing of the past. "Oh, it is wonderful."

Many of their older grandchildren, after marriage, took honeymoons or vacations at the Lake Arrowhead Hall's home. This ten-year period is an amazing time in our family's history.

My mother got more into decorating at Christmastime than she ever had before, which was a great deal. The upstairs narrow loft with an opening to the street shone with the perfectly decorated Christmas tree. We had some family celebrations there with the entire group.

These long-awaited worry-free happenings were greatly appreciated by their children, especially.

My parents were quite popular in the Lake Arrowhead Ward, especially when my father was called as a bishop. We heard what an inspirational and humorous speaker he was. And, surprising to me, he was great with the youth. They would line up outside the bishop's office on Sunday to receive counsel from him. My father? Yes. "Oh, it is wonderful."

Telling me what great insight my father gained as a bishop was like a nutritious food for my soul. He said one time, a couple came in pleading for counseling, and after they had a prayer, he felt inspired to give them some advice. He thought to himself, *Wow, I'm good.* But then immediately, it was almost as if he felt a knock on the top of his head reminding him that the mantle of bishop was placed upon him when he was set apart. The inspiration he received that evening was from the Lord.

Once, as my family visited my parents in Lake Arrowhead and went to church, we decided we would sit in one long row near the front. When Bishop Hall got up to speak, after the sacrament was passed, we all put on sunglasses, stared at the bishop, and did not crack a smile. He kept talking and not even glancing our way as he would have undoubtedly lost his composure. It is a hilarious moment we will all remember. (But I do not recommend anyone else do that, of course!)

Always having had problems with her feet and knees as well as a curvature in her spine for as long as I could remember, I watched my mother as she kept in motion but showed signs of pain. At this point, trying to do workouts or walk long distances had become a thing of the past. However, there were still occasions when she and my father would dance. They both enjoyed various kinds of music and loved to "cut a rug." This passion was passed down to all of their children.

My father did love his toys, such as boats, trucks, cars, and motorcycles. His two counselors also loved to ride motorcycles. They would all three ride to visit members. Once, two new single sisters took an unusually long time to open the door to these three men with motorcycle jackets on holding their helmets who claimed to be the bishopric!

The temple assigned for their ward's district was the Las Vegas Temple. That was quite a distance, but both of my parents went often. My father used to jokingly tell me he hoped he would be blessed in the next life according to all the miles he put on his vehicles going "down the hill." The most memorable occasion was when my sister went through for the first time to the Las Vegas Temple. I thought and felt what a sweet moment in our family's life that was. The Spirit hit me more powerful than ever before in the temple when I saw her walk into the Celestial Room. All six of us were there together. My tears were uncontrollable, and I felt a bit embarrassed. But what a beautiful blessing that was.

*What is the remedy? The first thing we must understand is that addictions are so much easier to prevent than to cure. In the Savior's words, "Suffer none of these things to enter into your heart." The best defense against addiction is never to start.*

*But what of those who find themselves in the grip of addiction? Please know, first of all, that there is hope. Seek help from loved ones, Church leaders, and trained counselors. The Church provides addiction recovery help through local Church leaders, the Internet, and in some areas, LDS Family Services.*

*Always remember, with the Savior's help, you can break free from addiction. It may be a long, difficult path, but the Lord will not give up on you. He loves you. Jesus Christ suffered the Atonement to help you change, to free you from the captivity of sin. The most important thing is to keep trying—sometimes it takes several attempts before people find success. So don't give up. Don't lose faith. Keep your heart close to the Lord, and He will give you the power of deliverance. He will make you free.*[1]

—Dieter F. Uchtdorf

[1] Elder Dieter F. Uchtdorf, "Are You Sleeping through the Restoration?" LDS General Conference, https://abn.churchofjesuschrist.org/study/general-conference/2014/04/are-you-sleeping-through-the-restoration?lang=eng&adobe_mc_ref=https%3A%2F%2F www.churchofjesuschrist.org%2Fstudy%2Fgeneral-conference%2F2014%2F04%2Fare-you-sleeping-through-the-restoration%3Flang%3Deng&adobe_mc_sdid=SDID%3D 7358C13F63B7BDDD-09A900D1501F5CEE%7CMCORGID%3D66C5485451E5 6AAE0A490D45%2540AdobeOrg%7CTS%3D165317368 9

# CRUISIN' IN STYLE

*To be a Christian means to forgive the inexcusable because God has forgiven the inexcusable in you.*[1]

—C. S. Lewis

As my parents were approaching their fiftieth wedding anniversary with no untimely bumps in the road (what a relief to us) to celebrate, we made plans to surprise them with their first cruise in the Caribbeans. The four of us chipped in and paid for them to have a luxurious balcony suite. This was a much-anticipated vacation for our parents and also thirty other family members.

A few of our children as well as nieces and nephews were onboard for this grand event. Our oldest daughter opted out because her firstborn baby was due one week before departure. And being late did not arrive until after we were on the open waters. I was disappointed that this grandbaby did not come on time. It had been a beautiful experience to witness some of the births of my grandbabies. Much different (and easier) than my own, of course.

I do not know of any other families to be as fortunate to cruise with so many loved ones. We felt particularly blessed. Eating together, dancing, attending talented shows, swimming, hiking, and snorkeling, seeing beautiful islands, laughing, and laughing, and laughing—has to be a top memory of the Hall family!

My parents' favorite excursion was riding in a submarine, gazing safely behind the glass windows at the underwater life. The whole cruise to them felt as if they were in heaven. They could be with family or eat delicious food whenever, and when they got tired of that, they could just go back to their cabin suite.

A highlight of our cruise would have to be an impromptu skit that the cruise director, Lenny, put together during one of the shows. He had an Australian accent and spectacular spur-of-the-moment sense of humor. Our family was a bit spread out in the audience, as seating thirty-two people together was impossible.

Lenny was looking for a young female to play the role of a damsel in distress. That was our Suzie! She about leaped over four rows of the audience when Lenny motioned for her to come on up. Suzie was not shy, an understatement. She took her bows immediately.

When Lenny asked for a villain, some nearby family members kept pointing to my younger brother Rick. Reluctantly, when chosen, Rick sauntered his way up to the stage as any wicked villain would, receiving many boos on his way. It was interesting that Lenny had no idea these first two stars were related.

Another interesting fact is that Rick did go on stage for several performances later in his life, managing and staring in tribute bands as lead singer and guitarist. His daughter sang on stage on the cruise and also sang in some of her father's bands later in life. When Rick was hired by a top-performing band in later years, our father was so proud of his son.

Back to the cruise skit. The hero was a stout older gentleman who fit right in with the other two thespians. He also took his bows as any hero would. Surprisingly, he was not related to our family.

About halfway through the skit, Lenny instructed Rick to let out a lustful moan as he spotted beautiful Suzie through the window. My brother kept a straight face for only a few seconds as he tried to remain in character. He finally busted out laughing. Lenny was confused and then Rick said in between gasping laughs, "But she's my niece!" This about brought the house down. But then Suzie had her moment to shine in a dying scene, which she leaned into for a good two minutes. We, as you can imagine, had no idea this was a foreshadow of things to come.

For the next two days, we wondered where Suzie had been. She barely came out of the cabin she was sharing with her sister. We were told that Suzie was glued to their cabin TV, watching the recorded skit of her debut over and over again.

Then finally the star appeared! She knocked on our cabin door and exclaimed as we opened it, "Mom and Dad! I had my ten minutes of fame, and I am good to go!"

In September 2001, after a week on our heavenly cruise, it was over. A few days later, the devastating 9/11 occurred. We felt thankful to have scheduled our vacation when we did, or we would have been stuck in Florida for who knows how long.

Less than six months after our memorable cruise, we received word from an officer at our front door that our twenty-year-old daughter, Suzie, had been in an accident and had not survived. She was now on her heavenly journey. That immediately stopped a Relief Society lesson I was preparing for the next day. I was Relief Society president, and Troy was high priest group leader. Instead of us serving others, others were serving us. I had the most challenging time allowing this to happen, so out of sync.

What do you do as a parent when you receive that kind of news? Denial, anger, what-if's, lots of tears. A lot of prayers. Also, gratitude for the knowledge of eternal families. Gratitude for Suzie's dream being carried out of being on stage before she moved on ahead of us. Irreplaceable memories for our entire family.

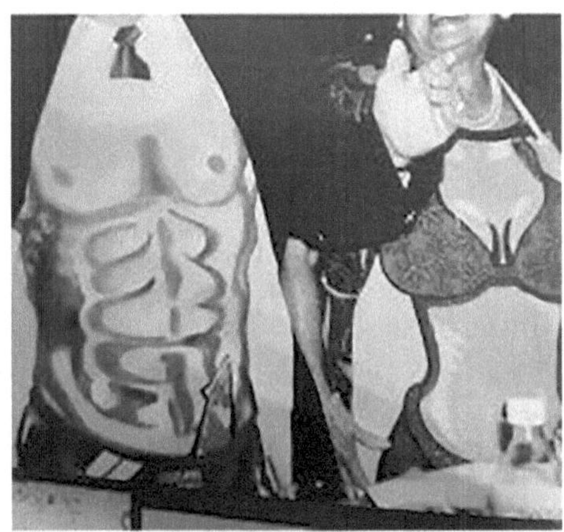

Our parents in silly aprons we gave them on the cruise

*Happiness in family life is most likely to be achieved when founded upon the teachings of the Lord Jesus Christ. Successful marriages and families are established and maintained on principles of faith, prayer, repentance, forgiveness, respect, love, compassion, work, and wholesome recreational activities.*[2]

—The Family: A Proclamation to the World

1   C. S. Lewis, "The Weight of Glory," ttps://www.reddit.com/r/Christianity/
comments/9gj9uc/to_ be_a_christian_means_to_forgive_the/

2   "The Family: A Proclamation to the World," https://abn.churchofje-
suschrist.org/study/scriptures/the-family-a-proclamation-to-the-world/
the-family-a-proclamation-to-the-world?lang=eng&adobe_mc_
ref=https%3A%2F%2Fwww.churchofjesuschrist.org%2Fstudy%2Fscrip-
tures%2Fthe-family-a-proclamation-to-the-world%2Fthe-family-a-procla-
mation-to-the-world%3Flang%3Deng&adobe_mc_sdid=SDID%3D0241
8F48CF77E098-573922D1E90FF199%7CMCORGID%3D66C5485451E56
AAE0A490D45%2540AdobeOrg%7CTS%3D1653253342

# ONE-SIDED CONVERSATION

As my mother's health was deteriorating, the harsh reality set in that they would need to move to a location better fit for her needs. It meant selling their beautiful home in Lake Arrowhead.

This must have been such a tough time, especially for my father. The housing market was not booming at the time, and they were not able to make much of a profit as expected. The plan was to land back in Arizona after my mother had two knee replacements while they lived in Blythe, California, in a trailer park near a medical center.

How poetic it seemed that my parents' beginnings in Arizona were going to be their grand finale. Since Troy and I had the largest family with all of our children living in the area, it seemed the most suitable place for them in their elderly years.

After my mother's first surgery, I visited them with one of my daughters. My mother was quite positive, which was her typical nature. We had recently lost our daughter Suzie, and I had been seeing a therapist for severe depression. Seems as if losing a daughter was the straw that broke this camel's back per se.

My therapist was also getting down to the painful part of my past that I had with caring for my siblings and parents and going through a rough divorce.

Before our five-day visit ended and I had been helping my father with caring for my mother, I was looking for the perfect opportunity to fulfill an assignment my therapist had given me. It is something I had thought of often doing since my parents were healed of the awful addiction to alcohol. I dislike confrontation and speaking of hurtful moments in my life. It is so much easier to keep moving forward, but this also means not healing completely.

I tried to get out of that assignment, saying I did not want to hurt my parents. After all, they were really old now. (Here I am around that same age, and I am not old at all!) It made sense as she said it was time for my parents to have that conversation to open their awareness, admit, apologize, and move forward. Our family was quite skilled at setting this topic on a shelf and allowing the dust to settle over it.

With my daughter out of their trailer for a while, and the three of us sitting around the kitchen table after dinner, I got up all the courage needed to communicate what had been on my mind and in my heart for many years. There were no distractions, no TV, just the precise quiet solitude I needed.

Here is almost word for word of the conversation:

"Mom and Dad, there's something I've been wanting to speak with you about for a long time. (Silence.)

"For around forty years, the two of you succumbed to alcohol now and then. I was younger than three years old when I first became aware of it but did not realize what was going on until about nine years of age. (Silence.)

"I know this is extremely difficult for you to hear, and, believe me, it is just as hard for me to discuss it with you. (Silence.)

"I'm sure proud of how you both have turned your lives around through repentance, and we love all these great memories we have been sharing with you both. I want you two to know how much I admire and love you as my parents. Yes, I had some tough times as the oldest child. (And still, silence.)

"Yes, it affected me. But here I am, most likely stronger because of all that. I like myself and where I am in my life. I have forgiven you both. I have learned so much thanks to you both. (Silence.)

"Thank you for making me a better and stronger person." (Silence.)

Yep, extended periods of silence from my parents as I poured out my heart and laid it on thick. I did not see a change in either of their facial expressions. Perhaps I totally caught them off guard, never expecting any of their children to mention this. It was a very strange conversation for me, but it did me the good I needed in a way. This one-sided conversation was not carried on by all present, but it was heard by all three of us. Neither of them ever brought it up in the years to come. Could it have been too painful for them to express their feelings?

*Closely related to our own obligation to repent is the generosity of letting others do the same... In this we participate in the very essence of the Atonement of Jesus Christ... We don't want God to remember our sins, so there is something fundamentally wrong in our relentlessly trying to remember others' sins... It is one of those ironies of godhood that in order to find peace, the offended, as well as the offender, must engage the principle of forgiveness.*[1]

—Jeffrey R. Holland

1   Jeffrey R. Holland, "The Peaceable Things of the Kingdom," Ensign, November 1996, 82, https://emp.byui.edu/SATTERFIELDB/PDF/PeaceableThi ngs-JRH.pdfElder

# BEGINNINGS FULL CIRCLE

Following my mother's knee replacements, my parents circled back around to Arizona, where their union had begun. This was the time period when my father began to lose weight caring for his beloved wife. Unfortunately, she had not fully recovered after both surgeries. It was not long before she began to experience hallucinations and loss of memory. It seemed that losing her ability to follow a recipe or play the piano was more difficult for my father.

It was a blessing for my parents to be near an enormous number of family upon moving to the Scottsdale, Arizona, area. And likewise, most of them were blessed to have them nearby. My parents came to all the family gatherings until my mother was not able. What a grand time all of their grandchildren here had getting to know and love them even more. Our youngest son graduated from high school, and my parents made it to the celebration in our home. There is a closeness my children gained from my parents that melts my heart.

As I realized my father's struggle to stay on top of his health while caring for my mother, I applied at a local agency as a caregiver for my mother. I was in the workforce still so I could continue to help our income and support my father and mother with their needs at the same time. Déjà vu. A significant difference this time (besides getting paid a little). This was a need not brought on by alcohol addiction. Oh, and there were no ATM payments under the door.

I saw firsthand that my father was the best caregiver for my mother, but it came to a point where he was not medically or physically able, so he searched for the perfect assisted living care center for his wife.

I remember three facilities my mother was in. When something was not in her best interest or seemed a bit "off" to him, my father moved her. He was with her every day and, thankfully, still healthy enough to enjoy her company to her last day on this earth.

My mother's personality never changed, even if she was in pain. She was a social butterfly, upbeat, and jealous of any female who thought to even glance my father's way. Some of these moments were only delusions. My father caught heck from my mother for that helper who was flirting with him. He always laughed it off. My mother was completely serious though!

My mother was diagnosed with mini strokes and was put on blood thinners. Seems to me the two knee replacement surgeries had taken a toll on her health more than they helped her. She only had a few months where she was ambulatory. The pain medications were of a high dosage to manage her discomfort. Most people would have been irritable, but she rarely showed that emotion. She was quite an inspiration to many of us.

I remember vividly the day before my sweet mother passed on to the *chosen other side*. I had two clients scheduled to work with, and by early morning, each had canceled. I decided to take advantage of that rarity and attend a temple session and then visit my mother. No regrets there!

The peace of the temple was needed to calm my soul. Visiting my mother was such a delight. All seemed exceptionally well with her. We laughed as we shared stories of happenings with family and in the world. She enjoyed her favorite pistachio ice cream and Diet Coke while I was there. That mother of mine was such a hoot! Of course, she mentioned to me how the caregivers there were all in love with my father. And she made sure to reiterate to them, "You can forget about him! Keep your hands off. He is all mine." No joking around then. All business in her mind.

I went home perfectly feeling content. By that evening however, my mother, age seventy-one, had gone downhill, having suffered from several mini strokes. The family was called, and thankfully, some were able to get here in time to say their farewells. She was kept comfortable with hospice but had very few moments of coherency throughout the next day. I am grateful I had followed a prompting to visit my mother the day before she passed away. Clients had canceled, which was out of the norm. It is a treasured memory. God once again had my back.

"Good night, Mom. I love you. Sweet dreams."

*God doesn't care nearly as much about where you have been as He does about where you are and, with His help, where you are willing to go.*[1]

—Jeffrey R. Holland

[1]  Elder Jeffrey R. Holland, "Created for Greater Things," https://www.goodreads.com/work/quotes/1520323 7-created-for-greater-things

# GRANDPA'S PAL

My parents had the cutest miniature poodle they named Sassy Boy. It was like they had another child. This was quite an amusement to the rest of us. It seemed my mother put up with this dog, but he did bother her. Sassy Boy had extremely potent gas. His favorite spot seemed to be near my mother. She always had the room spray within her reach too. She would grumble to Sassy Boy, "Why do you always have to sit by me? Stinky dog!" She did love him though.

I could see my father becoming more attached to his fur child Sassy Boy after my mother passed away. By this time, he lived in a two-story home on a manufactured lake that a family member had purchased. It was a beautiful scenic property, yes, in Arizona.

The stairs were an issue for Sassy Boy. The little dog was aging and having hip problems as miniature poodles tend to have in old age. My father had a back problem and was also beginning to have difficulty with the stairs.

Many years previously, when Sassy Boy was having problems with a leg, my mother insisted that my father give him a priesthood blessing. I was not told about this until years later. My father was a bit embarrassed but admitted the blessing helped. It was most likely the faith of my mother that enhanced that blessing for Sassy Boy.

All of us, when visiting my father in this lovely home, knew it would not be long until Sassy Boy would have to be put down. He also had vision problems. At this same time, my father was diagnosed with macular degeneration, something his grandfather had had and went completely blind before age seventy, I believe. My father's right eye was damaged, but he still had peripheral vision. He was handling driving well so far, having an automobile, golf cart, and motorcycle.

His longest trip would be to the cemetery and back to visit his wife. He kept fresh silk flowers on hers and our daughter Suzie's grave.

Some days, I would take grandchildren I was tending to, or clients with special needs, and my father would take us for a spin around the lake on his pontoon boat. It was not the Cathy-Lou but did fulfill his love of boating and the water. A couple of the girls I worked with on habilitation goals thrived doing activities such as this with "Grandpa."

About one year after my mother had passed away, as I was leaving a doctor's appointment, my father called me on my cell phone. He sounded distraught and did not make a lot of sense. Something about it will be better now for Sassy Boy. I was totally floored when I finally surmised that he had Sassy Boy put to sleep! I started to cry and asked him why he did not call me to go with him. "Why didn't you let me know?" His response was he knew he had to, and it was his job, nobody else's. I think he might have wondered if I would have tried to talk him out of it. He loved that little dog, and now the one alive connection he had with his wife for years was gone. One plus was that my father no longer needed to buy extra room spray.

My father did have two more dogs, but he was not as close to them as he had been to Sassy Boy. And there was a link shared with my mother through Sassy Boy, we believe.

His pets kept him busy, at least, and going on walks outside. Once they became too much of a chore for him, he let them go to another owner and knew they were happier getting more love and attention.

*Trust in God's timing.*[1]

—Neal A. Maxwell

1    Neal A. Maxwell, "Lest Ye Be Wearied and Faint in Your Minds," Ensign May 1991, 90. April 1991 General Conference

# EIGHTIETH SURPRISE!

Nearing my father's eightieth birthday, I thought it would be a grand event if several family members could surprise him. We reached out to many relatives who lived out of state, giving them a two-month notice. Andrew was able to contact a retired assistant manager who had worked for my father in Imperial Beach, California. He drove up with his wife, who had also worked in the thrift store.

We had Mexican food catered as that was my father's favorite. Two of our children began working on putting a hard-covered book together with pictures and special memories from family that was sent in.

I had anxious butterflies in my stomach the day before as my father thought this was just a small party with our family in the area. I was really excited to see the look on his face when people would start to appear before his unsuspecting eyes.

We held this in a clubhouse of one of our children's home-owners' associations. This way, it was big enough and easy to place decorations for the memorable surprise. All of our children helped, including a daughter-in-law who made special cakes, to make this a complete success for their grandfather.

All of our nearby family told him, "Happy birthday!" Then my father was instructed to sit in the birthday boy's seat.

One by one, individuals from out of town walked in to surprise him. Relatives from Oregon, New Mexico, and Idaho gave him quite a shock! He was in total awe and his look is a priceless memory. You would never have guessed this man ever had any addiction problems. "Oh, it is wonderful."

One of the funniest things that happened at my father's eightieth birthday party was when his past employee and wife walked in.

My father was puzzled. His eyesight was diminishing, so that did hinder his guess. He was thinking about family members, and we finally told him who it was. They had a great reunion as it had been several years since being in contact. I am sure they both looked much older!

*When you forgive, you in no way change the past—*
*but you sure do change the future.*[1]

—Bernard Meltzer

[1] https://quotesia.com/bernard-meltzer-quote/73168

# ROUGH SPOTS OF AGING

As my husband, Troy, and I were preparing to retire from our jobs, we gained inspiration after many prayers to put in paperwork to serve a senior couple's mission. Surprisingly to us, my father was not all in for us to serve a mission. He even stated to me, "Well, I hope they let you come home for my funeral."

Another concern of his was he would rarely get to speak with us. I assured him that a senior mission is different from when his young sons served. Promising to call him every day is something I lived up to until the day he passed away. A lot of those times when I called him while we were on our mission, he would tell me he had to go as he was watching something entertaining on TV such as *The Bachelorette* or mostly sports. The TV became a less lethal addiction. We all have our vices.

My father, at this time, was still driving. He was pretty content in his new independent living apartment. He had friends he thoroughly enjoyed there. Also, a benefit to this community was that they had enough members of the LDS church to hold Sunday sacrament meetings and also family home evenings on Mondays.

I realized my father was not social like my mother, but he thrived once he got in that situation. His friends appreciated his unique sense of humor. At this point in his life, he removed all filters. Our older children would tell us that Grandpa is allowed to say what they are thinking.

Because women statistically outlive men, my father had plenty of women after him. He had opportunities to date but chose not to. Going to lunch a few times with some was only for the tasty food, he would tell me. And he mentioned that he felt sorry for some of them.

Whenever my father asked me to, I would take him to a doctor's appointment to help with communication. There was also an amazing gal who was a caregiver to her parents and his friends two doors down from his apartment. When there were doctor visits made for all three, she would drive and accompany them to see their doctors. She worked for a caregiving agency which meant we could trust her. However, this job of the three elderly individuals was not a paid job for her.

For about six years or more, my father was given a narcotic prescription for fentanyl patches. While living in Lake Arrowhead, he had fallen on the icy snow and injured his shoulder. Pain medications were prescribed from that time on. He also had back and hip problems which caused severe pain.

When fentanyl became recognized as a dangerous drug, my father was informed that the doctor could no longer legally prescribe this. His attitude was, Why take an old man's relief from him when he was going to die soon anyway? This was a challenging time for him as he went through withdrawals taking a less strong narcotic. Still, a narcotic that has to be monitored carefully.

About one month after Troy and I had been serving on our church mission in Oklahoma, my father had a hernia repair.

I am thankful that my niece, a nurse, came to stay with him. He recovered fairly quickly.

After serving eleven out of the eighteen months we had been assigned to serve on our church mission, COVID-19 hit, and most seniors, including us, were sent home. Not our choice, as we had been reaping the rewards of helping preach the Gospel of Jesus Christ. After living in our home for almost one year, our youngest son and his family found an apartment to move into just one day before we returned.

Because of the pandemic, it was the beginning of tumultuous times for many. I became my father's advocate and health caregiver/advisor. And being the overanxious person he is, he was highly worried about the what-ifs. His health was deteriorating more quickly, especially his eyesight. Having macular degeneration, the sight in his right eye was almost gone. As he was terribly frightened about

COVID-19, I made sure he was vaccinated and had his booster, but it still hindered his optimism.

One of the most difficult things was when my father realized he needed to stop driving. At this point, he had sold his golf cart and motorcycle. His car was the last object of his manly dignity. It was a 2000 Ford Crown Victoria LX with only sixty-two thousand miles. He was appeased just to see it sitting in the assigned covered parking area, or one of us driving him in it.

After a couple of months of his "dignity" just sitting, my father relented and sold his car to a granddaughter who lives in the area. (I would not be surprised if he shed tears.) Her responsible teenage son now drives it and is enjoying the attention from his friends driving this classy vehicle. I once again felt great empathy for my father, who went from driving a car to sitting and maneuvering a scooter.

At two different doctor appointments that I took my father to, he was asked, "You don't smoke, do you?"

His reply was, "I have in the past off and on." That doctor, who happened to be a member of our church, was wide-eyed at that answer.

Another time, a different doctor asked, "You don't drink, do you?"

My father answered, "I used to. But it's been years." Another surprised doctor. I felt my father had made headway at being honest. In the past, he had always answered no to those questions. I respectfully ignored it.

Last year my father was upset that one of our adult children, who has two older children at home still, had left them at home alone overnight. The nearby neighbor was aware. I stated that he and my mother had done that, but many times more than just one night. And we were several years younger than our grandchildren are now. His reply was, "Well, uh, yes, you are right. I suppose we did. But things were simply different back then. We couldn't get in trouble." I knew if I went into it, we might end up in an argument, so I did not pursue that.

I felt more heartfelt compassion for my father these last three years than I ever had. He had been without the love of his life for over thirteen years when he passed away. Confusion set in, especially after two more moves into different assisted living apartments within one year. This way of living was always his choice, to have his privacy and some independence. It was a concern, though, when my father called for an ambulance twice instead of pushing his alert button.

Using the phone was an ongoing challenge. He could not see numbers on the home phone. We tried over and over and over again to set his cell phone on pictures of people. He could delete all of the things we put on there within the day though. How frustrating for him and for us.

Breaking two ribs and a sternum after one fall put him in the hospital, as well as a blockage another time, and then severe pain one last time. I would be able to rest easy then, knowing he was being taken care of. Of course, we would visit and stay when allowed.

It was truly a godsend that our children were nearby to help when possible. He told me often that he thought of them like his own. One daughter took him out about every five weeks to get a haircut from a regular barber. He sure anticipated those appointments.

Calling me instead of me calling him became the norm. Somehow, he could always figure out how to call me. I suppose I should be grateful, but these were tough times. It could be 2:00 a.m. when he would call to complain, and he would think it was noon. What happened to his lunch? I am not looking forward to growing up.

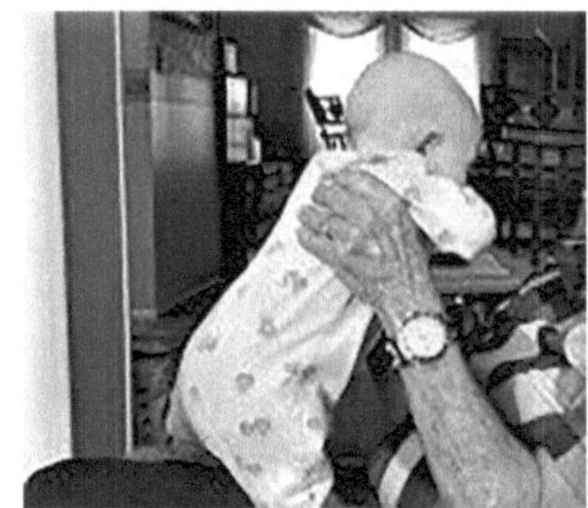

Nathan enjoying great-grandbabies

*O how great the goodness of our God, who prepareth a way for our escape from the grasp of this awful monster; yea, that monster death and hell, which I call the death of the body, and also the death of the spirit.*

—2 Nephi 9:10

*O how great the plan of our God! For, on the other hand, the paradise of God must deliver the spirits of the righteous, and the grave deliver up the body of the righteous; and the spirit and the body is restored to itself again, and all men become incorruptible, and immortal, and they are living souls, having a perfect knowledge like unto us in the flesh, save it be that our knowledge shall be perfect.*

—2 Nephi 9:13

# MONUMENTAL 90

Most days felt as if I was living on the edge of a cliff with my father's care and needs as he aged. Unless you have gone through this with a loved one, you cannot understand. As a youth, I felt on edge as well, not knowing with each passing day if my parents would change to their *other side*. Yes, different, but the feeling of helplessness I felt now and then was similar. It clearly seems to me that because of my past, I held triggers. These led me to feel depressed, anxious, and have a loss of appetite at times.

Struggling to keep love and forgiveness in harmony has been ongoing. The days that I managed to reach out in prayer to a loving Heavenly Father helped me to let go of some of that load. The scales would start to tip as one side outweighed the other. I struggled to feel love for my parents and feeling their love for me at times. I knew it was there, but feeling it was beyond my capacity as a weak human. Only through the Savior's love for me was I able to carry on and have hope. His Atonement on my behalf made it possible for me to completely forgive. He carried that load for me.

In my father's old age, I recognized his health conditions prevented him from caring for himself completely. It was heart-wrenching at times. The falls, the odd phone calls, memory loss, his rude remarks to me or about me to others. However, I had greater empathy for the state he was in now versus the state of being intoxicated many times in his younger years. I will not sugarcoat those forty years. It was agonizing sometimes and brought me to tears.

Keeping things positive for my father and his posterity was imperative to me. We planned a big ninetieth birthday bash for him. I spent more than a year taking notes as he related to me his life story. At the same time, he would give me his wishes for his funeral program. That would make things easier for all when that came to pass. My father's life story was included in a book I had printed out for his ninetieth birthday and given to all of our children and other relatives.

I came to recognize how important his accomplishments were to him. His family lived at the poverty level for most of his growing-up years, but he was trained not to show it. Thus the high level of pride he had. Some things seemed so silly even to him. My father would not walk out to get his mail if he had the same shirt on as the day or two before. What if a neighbor had seen him in that recently?

I had always wondered why it was so difficult for my parents to give compliments, and perhaps it was because they wanted perfection from their family. Hugs were not on their to-do list either. But as all of our family surrounded my father with love and hugs, I noticed he was coming around the last few years. I could say "I love you" every time I left his place, and he would repeat it back to me on occasion. Headway! But I know he was proud of his children and grandchildren because some of the caregivers would hear about it, mentioning it to me.

Not everyone could attend my father's ninetieth birthday party. Rick had been out to visit a few months before, so was not able to come again so soon. A few grandchildren were missing as well. I could tell he was enjoying seeing his posterity get along.

Andrew and I skated a happy birthday sign out to my father, and he was highly amused. Another highlight was Andrew and his wife composed a meaningful song for my parents, with Rick and two grandchildren playing accompaniment and singing along. It was made into a video with monumental life pictures of my parents and their family.

We made his favorite dessert, pineapple carrot cake, my mother's recipe, to go with club sandwiches. I hired a photographer to take group shots. We all agreed this special birthday was a hit with the oldest guy in our family!

# OUTLIVING MOST

We have seen more deaths these last two years than any others. Most were not even COVID-19-related. Several of my parents' siblings were in those numbers. My father outlived most of them.

Nathan visiting his wife's graveside one year before his passing

Backtracking to February 7, 2021, when a flood of emotion washed over me that my father would not be with us much longer. It seemed surreal. I immediately sat down at the computer and typed this poem out:

# DAD'S FINAL SEASON
## A New Beginning

We see him now—

His once broad shoulders

Now narrowed and frail.

His once straight posture

Now painfully stooping.

His loud boisterous jokes,

Now hushed and unfiltered.

His once strong spirit

Now larger than any man.

His once love for his family

Now deeper than the ocean floor.

His immense faith in God

Now closer to heaven.

We will miss him soon

Until our Final Season,

And New Beginning arrives.

Because of the looming closure of an assisted facility, we had moved my father to only eight months previously, we were moving him yet again. He was at the new place for only one month before he passed away. It was a stressful time for all. But this new place had more space, one bedroom with living room and a full kitchen. The access to visitation was tenfold easier for the family to come. He was on the ground floor near an entrance. Whereas before, he was on the fourteenth floor and a long walk down a hallway to his studio-size apartment. The visiting rules were also less stringent.

That last week of my father's life was a special time for him, I believe. Hospice took over and kept him comfortable. He no longer cared about TV or being able to use his cell phone. Relatives and other caring individuals flooded him with an outpouring of compassion and love. He had moments of awareness, and what a miracle that was for him and his visitors. Peace was there.

*And I do this for a wise purpose; for thus it whispereth me, according to the workings of the Spirit of the Lord which is in me. And now, I do not know all things; but the Lord knoweth all things which are to come; wherefore, he worketh in me to do according to his will.*

—Words of Mormon 1:7

# SPECIAL SPIRITUAL CONNECTION

My father may have had a tough time complimenting me, but I knew with his actions that he was proud of me and loved my husband and our family. He also understood and was grateful of the career I had chosen, working with those with special needs. I made sure he had a few copies of the books that I had previously written on hand that I wrote to give to his friends. There were also times when I cared for various individuals with unique needs that we would visit him. To all of them, he was "Grandpa."

One of these special gals was Ms. Meri. She was an unofficial but important member of our family for twenty years. She had only one older sibling. A few years ago, her father passed away within a few months after colon cancer was detected. Ms. Meri's mother was left alone basically to give 24-7 care to her daughter with Down syndrome and now had dementia.

Troy and I went to Hawaii and shared a time-share with Ms. Meri and her mother a few years ago. My mother had passed away about nine years previously. We would do our own thing there, such as canoeing and hiking. Since Ms. Meri needed to spend most of her waking moments in a wheelchair, her mother ensured they did not overdo activities. They enjoyed sitting on beautiful beaches and shopping.

One such shopping trip created a mystery for a while. Ms. Meri insisted that Grandpa, my father, needed this hula girl. Her mother relented but did not understand the urgency. Upon showing me later, I was also at a loss. We figured we would never understand the mindset of Ms. Meri. She would just repeat, "Grandpa needs this!"

Being inquisitive, I decided to call my father from Hawaii and tell him about the amusing incident. I sent him a picture via cell phone, which he could not see very well because of his damaged eyesight. I explained to him that it was a tiny hula girl who wiggles when sunlight hits it. He asked, "How did she know? Did you tell her?" I had no clue about what he was talking about.

My father explained to me that in the late 1980s, he and my mother made their one and only trip to Hawaii, and my mother bought a tiny hula girl figurine that moves when sunlight shines on it. In his most recent move, it was lost. I had never seen it. He was saddened by the missing memento that had been so special to my mother.

I explained to my father what had happened, and he said that I must have mentioned the missing hula girl to Ms. Meri. I assured him I had never seen or known about the little hula girl. What a blessing it was to have Ms. Meri close to my mother in a spiritual sense to receive guidance to buy my father this special gift.

*The Father is at this moment aware of you, your feelings, and the spiritual and temporal needs of everyone around you.*[1]

—Henry B. Eyring

[1]  Henry B. Eyring, "His Spirit to Be with You," Ensign or Liahona, May 2018, 88, April 2018 General Conference

141

# IT ALL WORKS OUT

*It isn't as bad as you sometimes think it is. It all works out. Don't worry. I say that to myself every morning. It will all work out. Put your trust in God, and move forward with faith and confidence in the future. The Lord will not forsake us. He will not forsake us... If we will put our trust in Him, if we will pray to Him, if we will live worthy of His blessings, He will hear our prayers.*[1]

—Gordon B. Hinkley

On February 2, 2022, I received the heartbreaking news that our sweet friend Ms. Meri, at age forty-two, had succumbed to COVID-19. Her mother told me that the whole time her daughter was in ICU the past few days, she not once complained. She was asking how everyone else was doing. No surprise there!

Her mother then asked if I would consider speaking at her services, and later that week, they told me it would be February 27. I agreed without hesitation. I felt honored to be that person to share Ms. Meri's sassy and loving attitude toward life with others. Her mother was very considerate of what was going on before that date as she heard my father was in the hospital again. I assured her that no matter what, I would speak at Ms. Meri's services. I had my notes ready within one week, so I knew it would all work out.

My husband, Troy, had given me a plaque years ago with the enlightening quote from President Gordon B. Hinkley. Troy had my number, all right! I would overthink and do the what-if thing, and that quote was as if President Hinkley were speaking to me directly.

Returning home from the hospital, my father was placed on hospice. The timing of his most recent move was miraculous as now his family would be able to visit him with ease. As mentioned earlier, we had barely moved him within the last month. The first floor, larger apartment, living room, full kitchen, backdoor access, and less stringent visiting rules allowed for his loved ones to spend time with him without complications.

All of our children and most grandchildren in our area went to tell their grandfather how much they loved him and talk about good times. Most also assisted in caring for him. I hope they realize how much I appreciated their help in my father's final days on this earth! Helping him eat and drink, moving him to get comfortable, bathroom needs, setting up a hospital bed in his bedroom, staying in contact with nurses—it lifted some of that from my worry plate.

My sister and her husband were here also from across the country during that time, which made a significant difference to my father and us. We made sure family could be with him 24-7 even though hospice care and nursing staff from his assisted living were on track. They were not able to be with him constantly, however. Not everyone was able to pick up and leave families and jobs, and we are appreciative of their phone calls and prayers.

The most tear-jerking visit for me was when our youngest son arrived with his wife to speak with his grandfather one last time. He began by reminding his grandfather of the dream he had had years ago where the family was climbing a large mountain, and his grandfather was in the lead with a rope, pulling everyone up. This was in relation to his grandfather being the head of the family, leading us all along on the right path.

Our son thanked his grandfather and reminded him that we would all be fine. We would miss him and still love him but would see him again. Then he began to play one of my father's favorite pieces on his phone since there was not a piano there, "Clair de Lune."

At the very second that tune began, I felt myself lose any control I had been mustering up the past week. Leaving the room at once, I became a basket case. I am not usually a crybaby, but that changed for a brief time. I was grateful that Troy was there to take me in his arms. I was blubbering and needed his comfort. My father would be gone soon, out of pain, such a blessing for him. And as for me, I would no longer be his caregiver.

Thinking back on this, that meltdown may have been saved up for years since my childhood of always feeling the need to be available if and when my parents needed me. I had felt responsible for their well-being for the majority of my life. Seems my flowing tears must have been emotions of sadness as well as relief. How would I even begin to process that?

Troy and I were at home when we got word that my father had passed away peacefully on the morning of February 27.

Of course, February 27. I was relieved for him, but it seemed surreal that he was gone from sight. And this would be a long day.

Seven hours later, we arrived at Ms. Meri's services. I was running on low energy but astoundingly felt I had spiritual strength that would sustain me. I had told all of our children to please not post on social media about my father yet. I knew this would cause worry for Ms. Meri's mother. But somehow, she had found out.

As we went through the mortuary doors, I was greeted with tearful hugs from Ms. Meri's mother. She was consoling me and apologetic. She knew I would not be up to speaking and assured me it was all right. I felt saddened for her having lost her daughter, and now she was feeling my pain as well. I told her all would work out, not to worry.

After Ms. Meri's brother gave a life sketch of his sister and how her life changed him for the better, I was up. It seemed sweet to me that his talk of Ms. Meri was similar to mine yet a lot different. It was a crowded house for the missed popular young lady.

I had not planned to mention my father's passing as I had my notes completed two weeks previously. Some of the memories I spoke about of Ms. Meri were as follows:

"I believe that God sent Ms. Meri here to teach us. I observed her parents learn great patience with all the ongoing care she needed. Ms. Meri had an extremely high pain tolerance. Whenever she said she did not feel good, it meant she had already suffered more than most of us could put up with. Ms. Meri was accepting of everyone, and we can all learn from her example to not judge others but love and care about them regardless. She had the ability to find joy in trivial things. A lot of descriptive words that describe Ms. Meri begins with an *S*, such as sweet, stubborn, sensitive, sassy, smiley, serious, and silly."

The last S-word I touched on describing Ms. Meri was "spiritual" and her connection with my parents, whom she called Grandma and Grandpa. I told everyone about the hula girl figure she instructed her mother to buy in Kauai because "Grandpa needed it."

And the next thing I know, in my conclusion, I felt a strong prompting to say something I had not planned on:

"My father passed away seven hours ago. I can picture Ms. Meri as she saw Grandpa, and she probably gave him a hug and asked, 'Grandpa, where is your motorcycle?' My parents had a special spiritual bond with that special gal. And I believe that will not end."

Ms. Meri on grandpa's motorcycle

There were a few tears as people heard my father had just passed away on the day of Ms. Meri's services. I felt an uplifted sense as I concluded my talk and stepped down toward my seat. But Ms. Meri's mother met me halfway, and we both were in tears as we hugged. She is such a compassionate and gracious woman. I had been so blessed to aid in caring for her special daughter. She taught me more than I ever taught her.

With my parents back together forever, it makes me smile to think of them dancing and working side by side again. My father endured over thirteen years without my mother. I am thankful that he is now free from pain and has a vision none of us can begin to imagine.

Now on to speak at your services. The harmony of love and forgiveness is alive and well, a grand blessing, because of the Atonement of our Savior Jesus Christ.

Good night, Dad. I love you. Sweet dreams.

[1] https://www.churchofjesuschrist.org/media/image/memes-gordon-hinckley-quotes-dfc4c3a?lang=eng

# TROY'S TAKE

In his own words:

Trixie and I had been seeing each other only a short while before we knew we had a real connection, and this was going to be a permanent relationship. Therefore, Trixie knew she needed to share the big family secret with me. What a bizarre conversation that was! As I listened in disbelief, I could see that she was serious. Her parents were and still are an overwhelming contradiction. They were beloved active members of The Church of Jesus Christ of Latter-day Saints and a pair of closet-case binge alcoholics.

The Halls were not your typical alcoholics. They did not drink every day, but when they would go on a binge, they would lock themselves in a bedroom and drink until fully drunk. They could stay that way for days or even weeks. Sometimes they would go out of town or hide out on their boat. Nathan and Anna must have struggled to keep this nasty little secret. After all, they were active LDS members, and everybody knows Latter-day Saints do not drink alcohol.

This news was difficult to accept. Brother Hall had been my teacher's quorum advisor many years ago. I could still remember the orange-and-green plaid blazer and green slacks he wore.

Trixie explained that this had been going on all of her life. This problem was also beginning to be a real concern for her and her siblings. In the past, her parents would stay intoxicated until they felt that they had had enough. Now they were losing what little self-control they had left and their ability to sober themselves up without outside help. And I was about to become part of this volunteer rescue team.

Trixie called her parents often. She would visit with them, but she was always listening for slurred speech or any other clues of an episode in progress. On one occasion, Trixie and her sister Lisa noticed that their parents had not answered the phone in two days. It was time to spring into action. Trixie warned me of what I was about to see, and I said I was ready. But I was not.

We went to the home of my future in-laws and knocked and rang the bell. When Nathan answered the door, Trixie entered the house and announced that it was time to sober up. Nathan looked up at me, and I saw shame and embarrassment in his eyes. Anna was indignant and retorted that it was unnecessary to bring me into this. Trixie disregarded any rebuttals or pleas on their part but went straight to work. Vodka was found in the kitchen, and she proceeded to pour the stuff down the drain.

We cleaned up for them, and they went to bed to sleep it off, or at least pretend to. Trixie then went home and left me to babysit her parents. The reader might remember this from the earlier chapter 19 entitled "Tag Team," where my brother-in-law and I both caught Nathan trying to escape and sneak off to the liquor store.

I love Nathan and Anna Hall. They have always been good to me. Early into my marriage with their daughter, I received a phone call from the bank. We were overdrawn because someone's check given to us had bounced. Trixie was at work now. I went to the thrift store where Nathan worked and explained to him our situation. I needed to put $20 into our account ASAP or checks that we had written would begin bouncing, each with a $15 penalty. Without hesitation, Nathan got out his wallet and handed me $50. Then he thanked me for coming to him first. Whenever I needed new (secondhand) clothes, he had instructed his thrift store cashiers not to take my money. Once when Trixie and I were moving, Nathan sent over a thrift store truck with two of his best employees to do the heavy lifting.

On some things, Nathan has been open with me. He was so disappointed with Trixie's first husband, breaking her heart and cheating on her. He so much appreciated me. He really did believe that his daughter would be in dire conditions as a single mother with four hungry children. He even thanked me occasionally for marrying his daughter. He had told Trixie that she was lucky to have found me, but he was wrong. I was the lucky one.

Nathan was fun to talk to. My own father passed away many years ago. Being close to my father-in-law helped fill that void in my life. He had a profound love of the gospel and a wicked sense of humor. It was amusing that he would call and ask me a gospel-related question, then tell me the raunchiest joke. We rooted for the same local teams. Perhaps we should not have, but we would poke fun at the same overly self-righteous individuals. He would tell the most hilarious stories of the half-witted employees that used to work for him in the thrift stores. Later in life, the social filters that should hold our inappropriate thoughts back begin to slacken. Oh, the things that came out of his mouth. In many ways, he reminded me of my own father.

On other things, Nathan was not open. I had personally seen him and Anna while they were intoxicated, yet they would not talk about it. When they were moving to Lake Arrowhead, there was some concern among their children about them being so far removed from their rescue teams. So many what-ifs. But, praise be to God, they finally overcame their addiction. However, they still would not talk about it, like the proverbial elephant in the room. I felt bad about this. I would have liked to ask questions. We know nothing of their turning point. The subject was somehow taboo. They just would not acknowledge it.

As for my wife, Trixie, she is amazing. I have had many conversations with her about her strange upbringing. Her struggles have cast an iron will and a ferocious determination to have order and consistency in her life. Trixie has serious difficulties relaxing when there is good that can be done. Her life revolves around giving service to others.

Seven hours after her dad passed away, Trixie was still able to command her emotions and speak at Ms. Meri's funeral. And not just dryly reading a statement; she spoke from her heart about a person so well loved. Knowing Trixie's pain, I watched in amazement as she had the audience laughing, crying, and bobbing their heads in agreement as she paid tribute to the deceased. Then when Ms. Meri's mom met her in the aisle and hugged her, the two of them openly wept while everyone in the chapel watched.

Two weeks later, she spoke again at her dad's funeral. Again, she had the audience laughing, crying, and bobbing their heads in agreement. Then it was time to get away. We went to Rocky Point and spent a whole week sitting on the beach, staring at the ocean. I love this woman.

Troy

# REPERCUSSIONS

There are many risk factors associated with excessive drinking. From my in-depth research, I have discovered that binge drinking poses dangerous consequences. These findings leave me with many unanswered questions with regard to my parents' health problems. My ex-husband's case is more apparent. The liver disease that took my ex-husband's life was diagnosed as alcohol induced. It can take several years or decades to develop liver cirrhosis. He was definitely on the lower time frame.

Excessive alcohol is the fourth leading preventable cause of death in the United States. Many accidents and deaths could be prevented. One example is Troy's ex-wife, who was driving while intoxicated which resulted in her immediate death. Thankfully, no one else was hurt. But sadly, her four children were left without a mother. Her two sons went to live with their father, who was a drug addict, in another state. Those two boys, now grown men, have been in and out of prison since their teens. It is quite tragic that they were not given love and the potential for happiness in life. Troy's daughters fared better as our home had a loving environment with consistency, and we held the best interest of the girls. They blended well with our six other children. At the time, our two oldest were grown and moved out. Like most blended families, we experienced some tough times, but we weathered it together, and our bond grew stronger.

Excessive drinking is detrimental to health and a leading preventable cause of death. Other diseases that excessive alcohol consumption can increase the risk of are brain damage, cancer, pancreatitis, and immune system dysfunction. Others which my parents suffered from may have been from chronic alcohol consumption or genetics. We will never know for certain.

Women should totally refrain from drinking while pregnant. I assume my mother did or at least cut way back. She had a miscarriage before my conception, but her four full-term babies were born healthy. When I worked in the special education field, there were siblings in the elementary class who were born with fetal alcohol syndrome. The young boy was being raised by his grandmother, and his sister was being raised by an aunt. They were vibrant children, ambulatory but nonverbal and developmentally delayed. They seemed to have unending energy! I witnessed the exhaustion of the grandmother, which was heartbreaking.

There are other health repercussions of heavy drinking which my parents may have suffered from. Before my father was thirty years old, he had an ulcer that was so extreme that doctors removed half of his stomach. Both of my parents suffered from bowel disorders, especially my father as he aged. But then again, many elderly individuals do. High blood pressure and high cholesterol were also health challenges they both had. All of these could have been consequences of their binge drinking. But then again, they could have also been genetically predisposed.

Because my parents were malnourished while binge drinking, they also suffered from a vitamin deficiency. This interrupted the bone marrow's red blood cell production, causing confusion and poor judgment. My father barely survived a two-week or longer binge. Feeling depressed and confused, my mother almost took her own life after a long binge.

The bone loss from chronic drinking in women is higher than that of males. Estrogen is depleted with alcohol consumption, which can lead to bone loss, fractures, and osteoporosis. My mother developed osteoporosis and suffered constant pain in her back, feet, hands, and knees. I know of none in her family (parents or siblings) that had osteoporosis. I could see the pain in her eyes and on her face as she kept on the move and rarely complained.

Heart disease and stroke are also high risks from excessive alcohol consumption. My mother suffered from ongoing ministrokes which led to her death at age seventy-one. Studies have shown that heavy drinking in midlife increases stroke risk more than diabetes.[1]

Still another unanswered question: Was this genetic? It seems unlikely to me. Her father passed in his midnineties from a heart attack, and her mother died due to kidney failure in her late eighties.

There are people who are genetically predisposed to alcoholism and have a higher risk of developing an alcohol use disorder. Wisdom dictates if you never take that first drink, you will never know if you would have been one of those predisposed to alcoholism.

1   https://www.medicalnewstoday.com/articles/297734#accide nts-and-injuries

155

# CONCLUSION

*Life is to be enjoyed, not endured.*[1]

—President Gordon B. Hinkley

Life is a learning process. And as tough as it gets, we should always find joy in it. That is why we are placed on this earth—to find joy! I have not always recognized the joy in my life.

At times it can be a daily struggle to keep moving forward. I imagine life's journey as climbing a ladder. Each step up the ladder helps me to stay focused on my goal of eternal happiness. It is okay if I am not able to move forward at times. There will always be moments when I get off-balance and catch myself looking back at mine or my relatives' previous steps where we slipped off a step. This can bring me sorrow, regret, and anguish. That is why President Thomas S. Monson has admonished us often to repent daily. I need that to give me spiritual momentum to continue my climb up the ladder.

I had a vivid dream while we served our church mission in Oklahoma. In this dream, I was sitting on the edge of my bed when my Savior appeared to me. The sphere He was in pure bright light, but it did not hurt my eyes. My Savior stood about two feet off of my carpeted floor.

I stared in disbelief in my dream as I did not feel worthy of this. My Savior reached into my realm and handed me his worn and dusty sandals. He did not speak verbally, but I recognized in his loving eyes that He wanted me to put His sandals on my tiny feet. Of course, I am going to do what my Savior requests. (I should always react this way.)

I tenderly took the sandals, knowing that they were too large for my feet. Putting the sandals on, I was amazed that they immediately conformed to my bite-sized feet. He motioned for me to walk. As I began to walk, I came to high mountains, oceans, and low valleys, but I was not afraid. I maneuvered with ease. I felt no fear and was in complete peace.

Then I woke up! That was such an incredible dream that I will always remember. It is a lesson I needed. My Savior has always been with me, especially when I have high mountains to ascend, oceans to swim, or valleys to wander in.

I have not always recognized that my Savior was with me in my life. My fault. The addiction my parents had for over forty years was a burden for me, and the Lord was aware and knew I would be all right. As I look back, I am able to spot many of His tender mercies in my life. His signature is all over that path. I am living proof that there is always hope.

In Isaiah 41:10, the Lord tells us, "Fear thou not; for I am with thee: be not dismayed; for I am thy God: I will strengthen thee; yea, I will help thee; yea, I will uphold thee with the right hand of my righteousness."

> When thou passest through the waters, I will be with thee; and through the rivers, they shall not overflow thee: when thou walkest through the fire, thou shalt not be burned; neither shall the flame kindle upon three. For I am the Lord they God. (Isaiah 43:2–3)

As we realize any suffering, such as the consequences of addiction, can be made right through the Atonement of our Savior Jesus Christ, we recognize that there can be *two levels of healing*.

> Oh, it is wonderful that he should care for me enough to die for me! Oh, it is wonderful, wonderful to me!

1   https://quotes.thefamouspeople.com/gordon-b-hinckley-4803.php

# READER'S REVIEWS

*Living with LDS Alcoholics: Healing on Two Levels* by Trixie Neal is a memoir that takes us through the life of Trixie and her experiences with her parents' alcohol addiction and recovery. She talks about her life growing up and how her actions shaped her life as an adult. Always having an unconditional love for her parents, as she gets older, she learns to help them and forgive them. *Living with LDS Alcoholics* is an easy and engaging read because you feel like you are reading a novel instead of a work of nonfiction. Trixie's wit is delightful, and her patience is astounding! I enjoyed getting to know her and her family, and I appreciate the chance I was given to learn about something that I have no experience with. By the end of the book, I was able to empathize with Trixie and her family.

—Brittany P. (former teacher)

Being a new member of The Church of Jesus Christ of Latter-day Saints and also a recovering alcoholic thanks to my Savior's Atonement, Trixie's memoirs have opened my eyes even more to how imperfect we all are. At first, I felt inadequate compared to other members of the church. But now I stop comparing and look at others in a different light. The greatest gift is that of repentance.

—Derick J. (mechanical engineer)